The Management of COPD
in Primary and Secondary Care

Available from M&K online store:

Books can be ordered at: www.mkupdate.co.uk

Routine Blood Results Explained
ISBN: 978-1-905539-38-3

Issues in Heart Failure Nursing
ISBN: 978-1-905539-00-0

Nurse Facilitated Hospital Discharge
ISBN: 978-1-905539-12-3

Interpersonal Skills Workbook
ISBN: 978-1-905539-37-6

Improving Patient Outcomes
ISBN: 978-1-905539-06-2

Management of Pain in Older People Workbbook
ISBN: 978-1-905539-22-2

Visit the M&K website for a full list of titles in print and forthcoming books.

Forthcoming titles from M&K:

The Clinician's Guide to Chronic Disease Management for Long Term Conditions: A cognitive-behavioural approach
ISBN: 978-1-905539-15-4

The ECG Workbook
ISBN: 978-1-905539-14-7

Obesity and a Scientific Approach to Weight Loss
ISBN: 978-1-905539-18-5

Legal Principles and Clinical Practice
ISBN: 978-1-905539-32-1

Microbiology and Infection Investigations & Results
ISBN: 978-1-905539-36-9

The Management of COPD in Primary and Secondary Care

An introduction

Edited by Dave Lynes

The Management of COPD in Primary and Secondary Care
Dave Lynes

ISBN: 978-1-905539-28-4

616.2
LYN

First published 2007

British Library Cataloguing in Publication Data
A catalogue record for this book is available from the British Library.

Notice:
Clinical practice and medical knowledge constantly evolve. Standard safety precautions must be followed, but, as knowledge is broadened by research, changes in practice, treatment and drug therapy may become necessary or appropriate. Readers must check the most current product information provided by the manufacturer of each drug to be administered and verify the dosages and correct administration, as well as contraindications. It is the responsibility of the practitioner, utilising the experience and knowledge of the patient, to determine dosages and the best treatment for each individual patient. Any brands mentioned in this book are as examples only and are not endorsed by the publisher. Neither the publisher nor the authors assume any liability for any injury and/or damage to persons or property arising from this publication.

The Publisher

To contact M&K Publishing write to:
M&K Update Ltd · The Old Bakery · St. John's Street
Keswick · Cumbria CA12 5AS

Tel: 01768 773030 · Fax: 01768 781099
Email: publishing@mkupdate.co.uk
www.mkupdate.co.uk

Designed & typeset in 11pt Usherwood Book by Mary Blood
Printed in England by Reeds Ltd., Penrith

Contents

About the contributors

Eric Brownrigg is a retired carpenter and teacher. Eric has assisted in the coordination of 'Breathe Easy' support groups and participates in various initiatives including research and Practice Development Unit accreditation.

Dave Burns RGN, BSc (Hons), MSc is National Training Manager at Respiratory Education UK and Senior Lecturer, Edge Hill University.

Pat Fairclough RGN, MSc is a lecturer at Respiratory Education UK and a Respiratory Nurse Specialist.

Karen Frankland RGN, RM is Short Course Manager, Respiratory Education UK

Carol Kelly BSc (Hons), PGDip, RGN is a Senior Lecturer at Edge Hill University and Respiratory Education UK. Carol was previously a Respiratory Nurse Specialist in Hertfordshire and Respiratory Ward Manager, Lecturer/Practitioner at Warrington Hospital in Cheshire.

Dave Lynes ENG, RGN, DPSN, BSc (Hons), PhD is Head of Education at Respiratory Education UK and Academic Lead, Edge Hill University.

Sue Meehan RGN, BSc (Hons) is a lecturer at Respiratory Education UK and was recently a Lecturer/Practitioner at Southport Spinal Injuries Centre.

Jenny Sparrow BPharm (Hons), MRPharmS, Dip Clin Pharm is a senior clinical pharmacist specialising in respiratory medicine at Aintree University Hospitals.

Foreword

Chronic obstructive pulmonary disease (COPD) is an enormous problem. It is estimated to be the sixth leading cause of death in the world and it also has a corresponding high morbidity.

This high prevalence means that it is important that healthcare professionals are able to diagnose and manage COPD. With the advent of new medications and interventions much more is now known about how to optimise treatment, and patients and their families are rightly entitled to have access to good quality care. The Healthcare Commission's 2006 report Clearing the Air indicated that, of people admitted to hospital with an acute exacerbation of COPD, an average of 15 per cent die within three months. There is also evidence to suggest that mortality in acute COPD is related to the availability of resources and specialist professionals, with mortality rates varying from nine per cent in some areas to 21 per cent in others, indicative of inequalities in care.

COPD is preventable and treatable, yet its low profile and late presentation means that many people are not diagnosed until the disease has progressed to a moderate or severe stage, where interventions are less effective. The education of all healthcare professionals is therefore essential in improving care for this patient group.

COPD is not simply a disease of the airways; it also has cognitive and social aspects and if care is to be optimised it needs to be approached holistically. This book addresses a wide range of issues and includes a chapter on the patient's perspective, written by a patient, which gives useful insights. It merits a place in the healthcare library.

Gill Hall
Chief Executive, Respiratory Education UK

Acknowledgements

I would like to thank my children – Andrew, Heather, Kate and Ann – for helping and encouraging me to develop a healthy learning environment at home, and my mother Eirlys for continual support during academic pursuit. I am also indebted to Anne Richards and Lynda Slater for their valuable reviews and to Gill Butler for assistance with images and layout. Finally, I would like to thank Respiratory Education UK for permission to use diagrams and images.

Chapter 1
Introduction
Dave Lynes

Chronic obstructive pulmonary disease (COPD) is one of the most common chronic diseases and it will soon be one of the five 'leading' diseases worldwide (GOLD, 2004). This may be because of increased smoking, especially in adolescents and women. Patients with COPD frequently consult primary care practitioners, and COPD is responsible for considerable use of hospital services. COPD is also a major cause of morbidity, because it can have a considerable impact on the lifestyle of patients and their families, causing reduced mobility, social isolation, depression and anxiety. Indeed when the impact of lung cancer and COPD have been compared by interviewing carers or patients (Edmonds *et al.*, 2001) it is clear that COPD patients are more likely to experience symptoms for longer than lung cancer patients, and have significantly worse limitations of activities of daily living, and physical, social and emotional functioning.

Many COPD patients also experience unique problems such as a sense of guilt due to smoking, and due to the impact that their disorder has on their family life (Robinson, 2005). Indeed interviews reveal that COPD has a big impact on informal carers and families (Seamark *et al.*, 2004). Carers can experience similar losses to those experienced by patients, such as loss of income, social interaction, family events and holidays. The strain on carers is clear and exacerbated by financial problems if the patient can no longer work. Many patients find themselves in a downward spiral of increasing social and economic isolation, boredom, depression and disability.

As chronic respiratory disorders affect mobility, social isolation is an important consideration. Approximately half of COPD patients leave their house less than once per month or never in the last year of their life (Elkington *et al.*, 2005). Patients often describe their loneliness and their frustration due to planned breaks, such as Christmas with families, being curtailed due to illness (Guthrie *et al.*, 2001).

Patients with COPD are also regularly depressed (Elkington *et al.*, 2004). When lung cancer and COPD patients were compared using Hospital Anxiety and Depression scale (HADs) scores, 90 per cent of patients with COPD suffered clinically-relevant anxiety or depression, compared to 52 per cent of patients with lung cancer.

Panic and anxiety are common, as are loss of personal liberty and dignity (Guthrie *et al.*, 2001; Robinson, 2005; Seamark *et al.*, 2004). It is important to remember that the panic and anxiety experienced in COPD can also contribute to breathlessness; indeed panic and anxiety can cause breathlessness even in the absence of respiratory disease. COPD patients have physical and psychological triggers for anxiety (Elkington *et al.*, 2004) and it is therefore clear that holistic management of breathlessness, or dyspnoea, is necessary. As Krishnasamy and Corner (Krishnasamy *et al.*, 2001) emphasise, effective therapy can only be devised once the nature and impact of breathlessness have been understood from the perspective of the individual experiencing it.

The fear of death is also common amongst patients with COPD (Guthrie *et al.*, 2001; Elkington *et al.*, 2005). Researchers comment that these feelings are often voiced in the strongest language such as 'what a way to go!' and 'I'm terrified' (Guthrie *et al.*, 2001). Often death from respiratory failure has been witnessed during admissions to hospital resulting in a fear of dying in addition to a fear of death. At the same time, many patients may be unaware that they have a chronic, progressive disease and may expect treatments to cure their symptoms completely.

COPD is, therefore, an illness rather than a disease – the impact on the patient is a result of physical, social, psychological, cultural and other factors rather than simply a reduction in lung function. This makes the management of COPD challenging, not least because COPD patients will inevitably continue to experience symptoms despite treatment and their condition will continue to deteriorate. Because of this there is a danger that patients with COPD will be seen as 'heart sink' patients, who have a self-inflicted condition about which the health professional can do very little. In fact, although many current treatments do not affect disease progression, it is possible to prolong a COPD patient's life and to considerably improve their quality of life. There is every reason to be positive, optimistic and enthusiastic when managing COPD.

This book therefore approaches COPD in a holistic manner, designed not only to address the physical needs of the sufferer but also to offer insight into the psychological and social impact of the disorder. It gives a succinct account of essentials such as the pathophysiology and natural history of COPD and pivotal aspects of assessment and management across the disease trajectory.

Designed as an introductory text for the qualified health professional, the book should also be a useful reference for more established respiratory care practitioners. It reflects current evidence-based literature, but it is reasonable to say that what constitutes up-to-date treatment is always an issue, and there are areas of contention related to the management of COPD. Moreover, the evidence base underpinning COPD management is rapidly changing.

There are many positive initiatives in the management of COPD, and these are driven by motivated practitioners from a range of disciplines. However, as Halpin (2005) suggests, in the UK, patients with COPD have been badly let down by the NHS over the past 30 years. Indeed there is evidence that survival chances are affected by geographical location and specific hospitals, and that this relates to practitioner expertise and the availability of resources (Elliot, 2003; Roberts *et al.*, 2003). In many cases patients have been misdiagnosed and under-treated and often blamed for what may have been considered to be a self-inflicted illness.

Neither patients with COPD nor their families are especially vocal, and, with this in mind, we owe it to them to make what difference we can. Perhaps this book can contribute by encouraging the development of high quality care for all patients with COPD.

References

Edmonds, P., Karlson, S., Khan, S. and Addington-Hall, J. (2001). A comparison of the palliative care needs of patients dying from chronic respiratory diseases and lung cancer. *Palliative Medicine*, 15(4), 287–295.

Elkington, H., White, P., Addington-Hall, J., Higgs, R. and Pettinari, C. (2004). The last year of life of COPD: A qualitative study of symptoms and services. *Respiratory Medicine*, 98(5), 439–445.

Elkington, H., White, P., Addington-Hall, J., Higgs, R. and Edmonds, P. (2005). The healthcare needs of chronic obstructive pulmonary disease patients in the last year of life. *Palliative Medicine*, 19(6), 485–491.

Elliot, M.W. (2003). Improving the care for patients with acute severe respiratory disease. *Thorax*, 58, 285–288.

Global Initiative for Chronic Obstructive Lung Disease (GOLD) (2006) *Global Strategy for the Diagnosis, Management and Prevention of Chronic Obstructive Pulmonary Disease*. Workshop Report November 2006. Bethesda: NLHBI/WHO.

Guthrie, S.J., Hill, K.M. and Muers, M.F. (2001). Living with severe COPD. *Respiratory Medicine*, 95, 196–204.

Halpin, D. (2005). Editorial in *Best Medicine: COPD*, ed. Kassianos, G., Halpin, D., Jones, R. and Gruffydd-Jones, K. (2005). Oxford: CSF Medical communications.

Krishnasamy, M., Corner, J., Bredin, M., Plant, H. and Bailey, C. (2001) Cancer nursing practice development: Understanding breathlessness. *Journal of Clinical Nursing*, 10(1), 103–108.

Roberts, M., Barnes, S., Lowe, D. and Pearson, M.G. on behalf of the Clinical Effectiveness Evaluation Unit, Royal College of Physicians and the Audit Subcommittee of the British Thoracic Society (2003). Evidence for a link between mortality in acute COPD and hospital type and resources. *Thorax*, 58, 947–949.

Robinson, T. (2005). Living with severe hypoxic COPD: The patient's experience. *Nursing Times*, 101(7), 38–42.

Seamark, D.A., Blake, S.D., Seamark, C.J. and Halpin, D.M. (2004). Living with severe chronic obstructive pulmonary disease (COPD): Perceptions of patients and their carers. An interpretive phenomenological analysis. *Palliative Medicine*, 18(7), 619–625.

Chapter 2
Pathological processes, aetiology and natural history

Dave Lynes

COPD involves progressive airflow obstruction, which means that the diameters of the peripheral airways become progressively smaller so that it becomes difficult and eventually impossible to breathe. A simple analogy is that of breathing through a drinking straw rather than a wide diameter hosepipe; the drinking straw makes it take longer to breathe in and out.

This may mean that it is possible to sit comfortably, but when walking a distance or up stairs it may be necessary to stop to catch one's breath because it is not possible to breathe in sufficient oxygen to meet the additional demand due to exercise. If a smaller diameter drinking straw is used, it is possible that one may be extremely uncomfortable at rest; indeed, it may take so long to breathe out that there may not be enough time for the lungs to empty before it is time to breathe in, leading to 'dynamic pulmonary hyperinflation'.

The drinking straw analogy is an oversimplification, as air can also become trapped in the lungs due to a loss of elasticity and collapse of smaller airways. Indeed COPD is a disorder that affects the whole body including the heart, kidneys and muscles. It also has cognitive and emotional aspects such as panic and anxiety which may directly contribute to the sensation of dyspnoea. Aspects such as panic and anxiety are discussed in Chapters 3 and 9 of this book.

This chapter is a basic introduction to the natural history of COPD, some of the pathological processes that occur and some of the causative factors. These processes are described in more detail and in an applied fashion in other chapters of this book

Presentation

The National Institute for Health and Clinical Excellence (NICE) (2004) states that COPD is characterised by airflow obstruction and that the airflow obstruction is usually progressive, not fully reversible and does not change markedly over several months. Unlike asthma, once COPD is established the changes are irreversible and the disease continues to progress so long as the patient continues to smoke. In healthy non-smoking adults, FEV_1 (forced expiratory volume at one second) will decline by an average of 30 ml a year. However, in the subgroup of smokers who develop COPD, FEV_1 decline is by an average of 70 ml per year. Some smokers will decline faster than this (see figure 2.1). (Fletcher & Peto, 1977).

Figure 2.1

FEV₁ decline

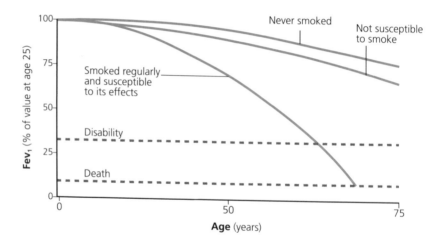

Importantly, significant airflow obstruction may have developed before the individual is aware of it. A substantial degree of lung damage can take place before any clinical symptoms become apparent and many patients with COPD may have a 50 per cent reduction in FEV_1 before they present to a doctor. This may be because we have more alveoli than are needed for gas exchange and therefore we can afford to lose a substantial percentage before dyspnoea becomes apparent (see figure 2.2).

As the degree of obstruction progresses it becomes more difficult for the patient to breathe, and airflow is limited, even during tidal breathing. The rate of expiration slows considerably, which can lead to dynamic pulmonary hyperinflation. When this happens, and when the patient has 'trapped air', the inspiratory muscles become inefficient and tire easily. This is because the diaphragm becomes flattened and the intercostal muscles are mechanically disadvantaged and use more energy just to perform their usual task of tidal breathing.

Figure 2.2

Lung damage can occur before symptoms become obvious.

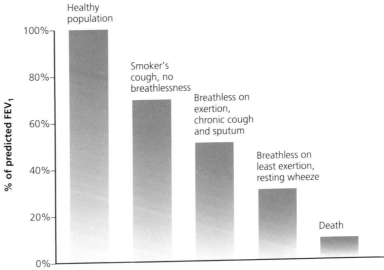

With increased disease severity, alveoli become hypoventilated and the patient becomes hypoxic. The lungs gradually lose their ability to oxygenate blood and exercise capacity becomes progressively reduced until the patient becomes breathless at rest. Eventually the patient will develop respiratory failure and, if they are significantly hypoxic, they will need long-term oxygen therapy (LTOT). LTOT can prolong survival if given appropriately (Medical Research Council, 1981; NOTT, 1980).

As the patient's lung function deteriorates they may exacerbate with increasing frequency, presenting with a sudden and severe worsening of symptoms such as breathlessness, sputum production and coughing. Exacerbations are frightening, distressing and disruptive for patients and they are associated with a worsening of prognosis (Seemungal, 1998).

Causes

Causes

The causes of COPD include smoking, occupational exposure to other particles, exposure to airborne pollutants, and alpha-1-antitrypsin deficiency. Risk factors include a history of childhood respiratory symptoms, middle and old age, genetic factors and socioeconomic status.

Cigarette smoking is by far the most important cause of COPD. A smoker may be ten times more likely to die from COPD than a non-smoker (Doll *et al.*, 1994), and there is a link between passive smoking and the risk of developing COPD. If children have persistent exposure to their parents' smoking they are likely to have worse lung function as an adult (Masi *et al.*, 1988).

Smoking irritates the bronchiolar wall. The body responds by producing additional mucus and the patient can develop chronic bronchitis. Smoke can also damage the respiratory bronchioles and the alveoli by attracting neutrophils which release enzymes called proteases. These enzymes can damage respiratory bronchioles and alveoli in susceptible individuals, which in the long term can result in the destruction of alveoli seen in emphysema. Some smokers will not develop emphysema, and it is probable that this is because they have an efficient protective mechanism against the enzymes that are released by neutrophils. Alpha-1-antitrypsin is an 'antiprotease' which is an example of a protective mechanism. A deficiency in alpha-1-antitrypsin can result in the early development of COPD, and may result in the development of COPD in a non-smoker. Alpha-1-antitrypsin deficiency is a rare condition which is probably responsible for about one per cent of cases.

The evidence related to the contribution of occupational and environmental factors to the development of COPD is less definite. This is because people who live in industrial environments also tend to smoke and may be exposed to passive smoking in their family or social environments. It is therefore difficult to establish the exact contribution that environmental pollutants make to the development of COPD. The incidence of COPD is certainly higher in industrialised and polluted environments than in rural environments, and it is probable that pollution from carbon, sulphur dioxide and other particulates may be responsible. These are produced by the burning of coal, fossil fuels and petrol.

Pathology

Pathology

The two main mechanisms that cause COPD are chronic inflammation of the small airways and gradual destruction of the alveoli (Barnes, 2002). The chronic inflammation leads to airways becoming narrowed, which causes reduced airflow.

Pathological processes, aetiology and natural history

It is important to note that the inflammation in COPD is different to that seen in asthma; it is driven by neutrophils (Barnes, 2000) whereas inflammation in asthma is driven by eosinophils. This has important implications for pharmacological management and prognosis, which are clearly different in asthma and COPD. While COPD is similar to severe, chronic asthma, in that both diseases are obstructive and therefore limit expiratory flow, in asthma the obstruction is primarily caused by a combination of reversible bronchospasm and sub-mucosal oedema. Some of the airflow limitation can also be caused by airway inflammation in its own right, as this results in plasma exudate, secretions, oedema and eventually basement membrane thickening. This airflow obstruction seen in asthma is usually at least partially, and often fully, reversible (see figure 2.3).

Figure 2.3

Asthma and COPD are both obstructive disorders and can coexist, but they are different disorders and require different pharmacological and other management. (Area enclosed by the dashed line indicates obstructive disorders.)

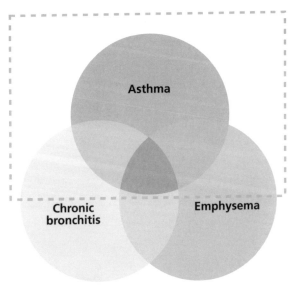

COPD is a heterogeneous disease, and affects different people in different ways, but there are some pathological processes that are common to most patients.

In the large airways, the mucous glands increase in size and number, which results in increased mucus production. The epithelium becomes chronically inflamed and breakdown of the integrity of the epithelium is often seen. The viscosity of mucus increases and the cilia that line the airways become destroyed. Because of this, the lung's ability to remove mucus is impaired, as the mucociliary escalator becomes inefficient. This is called chronic bronchitis.

In the medium airways, the airway smooth muscle becomes thickened and excessively contracted, which reduces the diameter of the airway. The small airways can become inflamed, oedematous and infiltrated with cells such as macrophages and neutrophils.

Smoking causes the neutrophils to release various enzymes such as 'proteases' and these digest and damage the alveoli. Inflammation also occurs within the walls of the distal bronchi and bronchioles, and this, together with the impact of repeated infections, leads to irreversible structural damage to the walls and sub-mucosa of the small airways (see figure 2.4).

This process can result in the destruction of alveoli and when alveolar walls are damaged they can coalesce, which means that some of the smaller alveolar sacs merge to become larger ones. Instead of small alveolar sacs that are highly elastic, the alveoli coalesce into large inelastic sacs. This is called emphysema.

Figure 2.4

Pathological changes in the airways

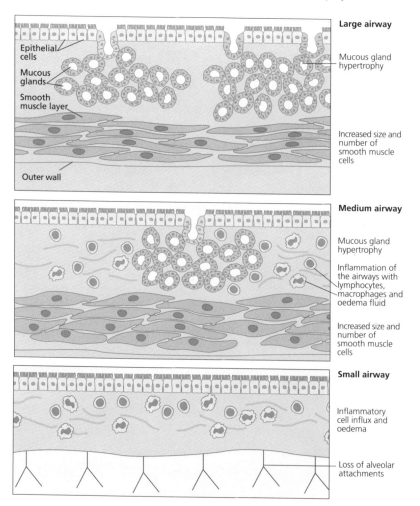

Large airway

Epithelial cells

Mucous glands

Smooth muscle layer

Outer wall

Mucous gland hypertrophy

Increased size and number of smooth muscle cells

Medium airway

Mucous gland hypertrophy

Inflammation of the airways with lymphocytes, macrophages and oedema fluid

Increased size and number of smooth muscle cells

Small airway

Inflammatory cell influx and oedema

Loss of alveolar attachments

This coalescence results in a reduction of the surface area of alveolar membrane, which results in impaired gaseous exchange. The smaller airways that supply air to alveoli have microscopically thin walls, and their shape and patency is maintained by attachments which act like guy ropes applying radial traction. Emphysema also causes a reduction in radial traction, which means that the small airways are not supported so they tend to close and collapse, especially during expiration. This will lead to air trapping, to increased work in breathing and to areas of the lung not being ventilated. Hence gas exchange is further impaired. This can cause a disturbance in the matching of ventilation to perfusion (see Chapter 7).

There are various patterns of emphysema but two distinct patterns have been described: centrilobular emphysema, which affects the proximal bronchioles leaving the distal ones relatively undamaged; and panlobular emphysema, in which the disease is diffusely scattered. If alveoli continue to merge they can form sacs that are larger than a centimetre in diameter. These larger sacs are called bullae (see figure 2.5).

Figure 2.5

Pathological changes in the alveoli and small airways

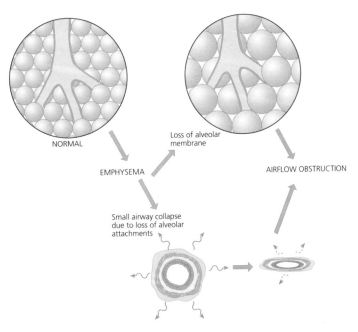

NORMAL

EMPHYSEMA

Loss of alveolar membrane

AIRFLOW OBSTRUCTION

Small airway collapse due to loss of alveolar attachments

Complications

Complications

Patients with more severe COPD can develop complications such as exacerbations, heart failure, and polycythaemia.

Acute exacerbations are significant events and need to be treated correctly. Their prevention is a theme of this book and it is specifically discussed in Chapters 5, 9 and 11. The management of exacerbations is discussed in Chapters 3, 6 and 7.

Cor pulmonale is right-sided heart failure, which is secondary to primary pulmonary disease. It is caused by increased pulmonary vascular resistance, due to hypoxia-induced vasoconstriction of the pulmonary capillaries. When alveoli are not ventilated they become hypoxic and blood capillaries constrict. This is the body's way of ensuring that blood passes over those alveoli that are ventilated, thereby facilitating gaseous exchange.

However, if hypoventilation of alveoli becomes widespread, and they become generally hypoxic, vasoconstriction of the pulmonary capillaries also becomes widespread. This means that the right side of the heart must work harder to maintain circulation, which can cause right-sided heart failure and pulmonary artery hypertension. Alveolar hypoventilation causes renal hypoxia which can result in ankle oedema and polycythaemia (an increase in the number of red blood cells). Polycythaemia increases the viscosity of the blood and may make the patient more likely to develop a pulmonary embolism. Cor pulmonale and peripheral oedema in COPD is indicative of a poor prognosis and it must be managed correctly. This is discussed in Chapter 10.

There is currently no cure for COPD and treatment aims mainly at controlling symptoms, improving quality of life and reducing exacerbations. However early detection, smoking cessation and correct management of complications can significantly prolong and improve the quality of a patient's life.

References

Barnes, P.J. (2000). Mechanisms in COPD: Differences from asthma. *Chest*, 117, S10–S14.

Barnes, P.J. (2002). New treatments for COPD. Nature Reviews. *Drug Discovery*, 1, 437–446.

Doll, R., Peto, R., Wheatley, K., Gray, R. and Sutherland, I. (1994). Mortality in relation to smoking: 40 years observations on male British doctors. *British Medical Journal*, 309, 901–911.

Fletcher, C.M. and Peto, R. (1977). The natural history of chronic airflow obstruction. *British Medical Journal*, 1, 1645–1648.

Masi, M.A., Hanley, J.A., Ernst, P. and Becklake, M.R. (1988). Environmental exposure to tobacco smoke and lung function in young adults. *American Review of Respiratory Disease*, 138, 296–299.

MRC (1981) Long-term domiciliary oxygen therapy in chronic hypoxic cor pulmonale complicating chronic bronchitis and emphysema. *Lancet*, 1, 681–686.

National Institute for Health and Clinical Excellence (NICE) (2004). Chronic Obstructive Pulmonary Disease: National clinical guideline for management of chronic obstructive pulmonary disease in adults in primary and secondary care. *Thorax*, 59 (Suppl. 1), 1–232.

Nocturnal Oxygen Therapy Trial Group (NOTT) (1980). Continuous or nocturnal oxygen therapy in hypoxaemic chronic obstructive lung disease. *Annals of Internal Medicine*, 93, 391–398.

Seemungal, T.A.R., Donaldson, C.G., Paul, E.A., Bestall, J.C., Jeffries, D.J. and Wedzicha, J.A. (1998). Effect of exacerbation on quality of life in patients with chronic obstructive pulmonary disease. *American Journal of Respiratory and Critical Care Medicine*, 157, 1418–1422.

Chapter 3
The patient's perspective
Eric Brownrigg

I was 16 when I smoked my first cigarette. My brother gave it to me in the bathroom as I was getting ready to go out. He was smoking one and said 'Have a puff on that'.

About 12 months later I bought my first packet of Woodbines. I was an apprentice carpenter and joiner and in the 1950s smoking was a social thing to do. Everybody smoked. Nobody thought it was harmful. We thought that later in life we might get a bit short of breath, but that was it. We had no notion that smoking caused cancer; cancer didn't come into it until the 1970s. Smoking was something that we just graduated to; all of our friends smoked and we just joined in with the crowd. I can remember sitting in class at night school passing my fags round to my friends. We could go through ten cigarettes each during one two-hour night school class. Smoking was acceptable in classrooms and just about anywhere else.

When I finished serving my apprenticeship I was called up to do my national service. I signed on shortly after for a period of three years, two served in Singapore. On returning home I was demobbed and, rather than go back onto exposed building sites, I opted to get a job in an office. I then worked in various offices doing accounts work until taking a job teaching. This was when I first noticed that there was a problem with my breathing.

At the age of 45 I became breathless halfway up a long flight of stairs and had to stop. By then I had been smoking for about 30 years. Gradually I began to notice other signs that there might be a problem. Part of my duties as a teacher was to give youngsters 'Social Education', which included walking to places of interest such as art galleries and museums. This sometimes involved two mile walks and I had to stop to catch my breath from time to time. I was quite a heavy smoker at that time, more than 40 a day, so for several years I just put my breathlessness down to smoking and age and I did not think that I had a disease. I simply thought that I should expect to be a little breathless.

It wasn't until I was about 60 that it became apparent to me that there really was a problem and even then it took another person to draw my attention to it. I guess I had become accustomed to being a little breathless. It was when I had my hip replaced and the physiotherapist noticed that I became breathless when climbing the stairs. She asked me whether I had seen anybody about my breathing, and I said 'No, I just put it down to smoking and getting older'. She advised me to see my GP. My breathing had probably been affected for 20 years before I visited my doctor about it and I delayed because I thought that it was the natural effect of smoking.

Difficulties in breathing, combined with the cost of cigarettes, prompted me to stop smoking and I managed to stop about 15 years ago. The cost was an important factor and I had been thinking of stopping for some time. Then I became ill with a bad dose of flu and that prompted me to stop smoking. It was difficult at first and I had to fight the urge to smoke, especially when I was with friends or family who smoked – I called this 'social pangs'. These social pangs persisted for some time.

Understanding my condition

**Understanding
my condition**

When I was first diagnosed and told that I had COPD I was unsure what it meant and I know that other patients are unsure because I have spoken to them at our respiratory support group, 'Breathe Easy'. In the first instance all I was told was: 'You've got COPD.' A couple of visits later one of the doctors said 'You've got emphysema, haven't you?' and I said 'Have I?' It was a surprise to me.

As time has gone on I have found out more. I have participated in some research studies and had CT scans, which have brought out the fact that I have a couple of bullae in my lungs. If I had not been involved with research, I don't think I would have fully understood what emphysema was. Emphysema, as I understand it, is a wasting of lung tissue. You don't really understand that just from the word itself. If somebody didn't understand what was going on with COPD I would recommend that they go to a support group such as 'Breathe Easy'. They have frequent medical speakers such as nurses and doctors. It can help when you meet other people who are experiencing the same sort of thing. You get to understand about inhalers – all of the inhalers currently in use. You may also get talks about what COPD is and get kept up-to-date with what is going on in the respiratory field.

Having COPD affects my life in many ways. I simply cannot do normal things. I tried to use a hammer to open a door recently but I was losing my breath very rapidly. I felt absolutely terrible because I knew that, as a carpenter, I should be able to fix the door, but I just couldn't. Sometimes I feel it's getting difficult to live with because I am not able to do the things that I should be able to do. I am very much a DIY-er, but I can't do it now. If I just pick up a screwdriver I get breathless. When I think about it I realise that not being able to do these things is a big loss to me. At times it makes me feel guilty – guilty because I can't do things that I ought to be able to do. I feel as though I let people down.

If I do any exercise, even playing a church organ, it is too much. Using feet and hands on the organ is too much. If I did not have a car I would be housebound or I would have to get a buggy to get around. I live about 800 yards from shops and bus services but if I tried to walk to the end of the street I would have to stop two or three times due to acute shortness of breath. My legs would also get more and more tired.

This breathlessness means that it is difficult to do things that most people take for granted. When I go shopping I'm fine if I can park near the shops and if the shopping centre is on the level. But if I have to walk or if there are any stairs it's a problem. It helps if there are places to sit when shopping. I know where all of the benches and seats are at our shopping centre – you get to know them.

Changing my lifestyle

Changing my lifestyle

Having COPD means that I have had gradually to alter the way I live my life. I can't do some of the things that I enjoyed doing, such as playing the church organ, and I can't socialise as much as I was able to. I used to participate in amateur dramatics – I've acted in musicals and plays – but I can't do that now. I do not have the strength or breath to do it. If I did not have COPD I would still be doing these things now. I loved playing the organ. I also miss the people that I mixed with – we had a good social life.

I have found other hobbies which I enjoy, for example I paint watercolours and I enjoy photography. It's not too bad if I have something to occupy myself, but it has to be something light. I get depressed and anxious occasionally, but if I can keep myself occupied this helps and generally there is too much going on to get anxious or depressed. Hobbies are a good way to avoid depression. My hobbies are not quite the same as amateur dramatics because they are solitary, but it is possible to meet others who share the interest. Recently I attended a week-long residential watercolour course and it was quite social.

I've learnt to try to modify where I go. When going on holiday my wife and I plan carefully. We make sure that we go to a place where there are no crowds and we avoid hills. The last holiday I had was in Mallorca and the promenade was only a few steps from the hotel. But at the end of the prom there was the choice of steep stairs or a slope and it took me four or five attempts to get up the slope. We can have holidays and we can have enjoyable holidays, but we are still quite limited with what we can do. The key is slopes. If there are any slopes or hills, I'm scuppered.

Exacerbations

Exacerbations

Exacerbations are an important part of COPD. If there is anything that can be done to reduce the number of exacerbations that COPD patients have, it should be done. Two years ago I used to have an exacerbation every three to six months but since then I have had a review of my medication and inhalers. Consequently I have not had an exacerbation for two years, which is fantastic.

Exacerbations are terrible. Anybody with COPD would dread them. They result in a complete loss of breath. I remember one occasion that was particularly frightening. I was attending the laboratories in the hospital and I noticed that I had to stop to get my breath. I tried to walk a little further but then I could not get my breath at all. It felt like I simply could not breathe in. I was looking at the nurses and the doctors but I could not speak and I was hanging on the doorway and trying to control my panic. I thought that the staff were not taking it seriously and it was making me panic but as soon as they took it seriously they couldn't do enough for me. If this had happened when I was out shopping I would have been completely stymied and would have had to be taken to hospital in an ambulance.

If a patient is breathless they need help straightaway; they need to be taken seriously. This is so important. If you want to imagine what it is like to have an exacerbation, pinch your nose and close your mouth and see how long you can do that before you panic. Don't give up when you feel like giving up, keep going until you become desperate and panic. If I was in a situation where I could not get help quickly that is how I would feel; I would feel this desperate panic. So if a patient is on a ward and they say they need help, this does not mean that they need it in an hour's time, they need it there and then.

I also feel that it is important to give COPD patients prompt appointments when requested. Recently I awoke with a dry cough, just a little rattle in my breathing and this non-productive cough. By coincidence I was visiting the hospital that day because I was taking part in some research about COPD. One of the doctors noticed that I was not myself and examined my chest. He started me on antibiotics and steroids immediately and over the next few days I became shivery and was producing brown sputum. However, thanks to my medication I was already starting to feel a little better. The doctor has since informed me that I had severe pneumonia, which was successfully treated at home and that the key to this success was early intervention. If I had had to wait several days for a GP's appointment things might not have turned out so well; I could even have died.

Dealing with chronic, progressive disease

Dealing with chronic disease

I realise that I have a chronic, progressive disease and that this means that my condition will gradually deteriorate. I understand that taking my inhalers will help slow the deterioration down and will reduce the number of exacerbations, but the disease will nevertheless very gradually increase in severity. There is not much I can do to change that; that is set in stone. I just have to accept it.

I deal with this in two ways. Firstly, I do as much as I can to put something back into the system so that someone in the future will benefit and there is a chance that we may be able to turn it round so that COPD changes from something that is chronic into something that we can do something about. This, amongst other things, helps give me a sense of purpose in life.

The second way that I deal with the reality of having a chronic disease is that I accept it. I realise and accept that my breathlessness will be there most of the time and that over time it is going to deteriorate. One of the things that brought this home to me is when I was shown a chart that compared the breathing of a normal person with how COPD makes your breathing deteriorate. Depending on when you stop smoking you go back to the curve of the non-smoker. Because I'm aware of that, I know that my breathing is going to deteriorate with age. I also know that, because I have been a heavy smoker, I have done damage to my lungs and they are going to deteriorate faster and I just have to cope with that. I can see that things have already deteriorated. When I was 45 I could walk for miles. Now I struggle with stairs. If a slope goes over five degrees I struggle.

Sometimes I deal with the reality of the situation by shelving it. I realise that my breathlessness is increasing but I will deal with that as and when and shelve it in the meantime. For now I will enjoy my water colouring and focus on the here and now. My father died at 72 from multiple myeloma and my mother died of cancer at age 82. I think that if I don't smoke and I look after myself I could make it to my 90s. I have just passed the yardstick, three score years and ten.

Meeting the needs of COPD patients

Needs of patients

It is good to have the opportunity to write this chapter because I think that it is important that health professionals and others understand what it is like to have COPD; if they do, then perhaps they will be more inclined to meet the needs of COPD patients.

Small things can make a big difference. For example, mobility is very important, and this includes access to transport and car ownership. Many people with COPD don't become disabled until they are over 65, which may mean that they may not be able to obtain benefits which would make a big difference to their lives. I did not claim for mobility until I was over 65 and I was turned down. However, if you claim before 65 you are still able to have the benefit after 65. Without a car I could not have a social life. Other small things such as priority parking spaces can make a big difference. A parking space would make a big difference to me because the parking situation near my house is horrendous. The lack of a parking space means that I am reluctant to go out, as I may have to walk from the bottom of my avenue, which is slightly uphill.

The patient's perspective

Recently the government has introduced a new initiative with GPs. This means that I occasionally I get a letter from the practice asking me to attend so that they can record my spirometry. I think that this sort of thing helps to ensure that people get the best attention and they need it.

Pulmonary rehabilitation should be available for all patients. I attended pulmonary rehabilitation and it was excellent. It was a course of 12 sessions and I came out revitalised. I was able to do more. I was able to walk a greater distance and found it easier getting up the stairs. Before pulmonary rehabilitation I could only get halfway up the stairs without losing my breath; afterwards I could get to the top.

If I could leave you with a final thought, it is that a good member of staff always makes a difference. When people suffer from a disabling, frightening disease the quality of nurses is very important. The most important thing is understanding. If healthcare staff can get some impression of what it is like not to get your breath they are halfway there.

Chapter 4
Assessment and diagnosis
Karen Frankland and Dave Lynes

The diagnosis of COPD can be difficult, and it can be especially difficult to differentiate COPD from asthma. COPD should be suspected when patients have signs and symptoms and the diagnosis of COPD is supported by spirometry but a COPD patient's lung function can diminish by as much as 50 per cent before they present with symptoms at all. Physical examination of a patient with early COPD can be completely unremarkable and there are likely to be no outward signs of the disease. Auscultation of the chest will probably reveal no abnormalities (such as wheezing), and the patient's pulse, blood pressure and resting respiratory rate may be normal. Yet spirometry may reveal that they are in the earlier stages of this progressive obstructive disorder.

If we can identify patients before they lose lung function and develop 'clinically significant' COPD, we can delay or prevent patients from developing severe COPD. Because of this, guidelines such as those from NICE (2004) have recommended that patients over the age of 35 who are current or ex-smokers with a chronic cough, and all patients with chronic bronchitis, should have spirometry. In fact, all patients with respiratory symptoms should have spirometry, and, if resources permit, it is arguably appropriate to screen all smokers over 35, although this is not recommended in current guidelines.

A diagnosis of COPD should be considered in patients over the age of 35 who have a risk factor (generally smoking) and who present with one or more of the following symptoms: exertional breathlessness, chronic cough, regular sputum production, frequent winter 'bronchitis' or wheezing (NICE, 2004). However it is important to remember that COPD is a heterogeneous disease – it can affect patients in different ways. Patients may or may not present 'classically' and a superficial understanding of the disorder and of the difference between it and asthma can result in misdiagnosis. The questions asked of patients during history-taking therefore only make sense if they are informed by an understanding of their rationale.

Even in more severe, established cases of COPD, where the clinical picture is less obscure, patients can present in different ways. There are two 'caricatures' of COPD – the 'pink puffer' and the 'blue bloater' – and you may encounter patients who present similarly to such caricatures. The pink puffer may be underweight, may gasp for breath, and may experience 'type 1' or hypoxic respiratory failure. The blue bloater patients may be blue and oedematous. But, in reality, most patients with more severe COPD will present with a combination of these features.

If COPD is early onset and associated with minimal smoking history, a diagnosis of alpha-1-antitrypsin deficiency should be considered. You may wish to consider counselling the patient before testing for alpha-1-antitrypsin deficiency, as there may be implications for them and their family such as increased life and health insurance premiums. Patients identified as having alpha-1-antitrypsin deficiency should be offered the opportunity to be referred to a specialist centre to discuss the clinical management of this condition (NICE, 2004).

COPD and smoking history

Smoking history

Smoking history is arguably the most important information to ascertain. It is not possible simply to say that 'if a patient has smoked more than 20 cigarettes per day for 20 years they have COPD'. Some smokers, even heavy smokers, may never develop COPD; approximately 20 per cent of smokers develop the disorder (Calverley et al., 2004). On the other hand, some people with a comparatively low smoking history may have COPD. People vary in their susceptibility to tobacco smoke because the lungs have defence mechanisms which vary in their effectiveness from person to person.

The number of cigarettes smoked is nevertheless an important factor and this is assessed by calculating the number of 'pack years'. One 'pack' is 20 cigarettes. The formula for calculating pack years is as follows:

pack years = the number of packs smoked each day
x number of years the patient has smoked.

For example, a woman who has smoked ten cigarettes a day for 30 years, has 15 pack years. A man who has smoked 40 cigarettes a day for 25 years has 50 pack years.

The pack year calculation is inexact because smoking habits vary; for example, some smokers may only smoke half the cigarette. Packs may also vary in strength and it is difficult to calculate the impact of rolling and pipe tobacco, with or without filters. Nevertheless, 'pack years' are a useful guide. The man described above may be more likely to have COPD because he has more 'pack years', although it is important to understand that the woman may also have COPD because she may be highly susceptible to the effects of cigarette smoke.

Recording symptoms of COPD

Recording symptoms

As COPD develops it is possible that the patient will wheeze, that they will develop a degree of dyspnoea and that they will cough and produce sputum. Individual patients may rank the importance of different symptoms differently but breathlessness is generally the symptom which causes them most concern. If COPD is suspected, the patient should also be asked about their exercise capacity, for example walking for a bus or climbing hills or stairs. It may also be appropriate to ask about their ability to work and engage in activities of daily living such as washing, dressing and eating. It is probable that the established COPD patient will have problems in these areas and will have a history of decline. Ask the patient about ability to perform particular tasks, including how long they need to perform the task. This information is especially useful when compared with the time needed a number of years ago.

The more severe patient may be initially breathless on exertion, such as when climbing stairs, and, as the disorder progresses, may experience breathlessness at rest. This is likely to increase with any exertion, such as making a cup of tea. More severe disease causes noticeable breathlessness at rest. At this stage of the disorder the patient may fix their shoulder girdles and use accessory muscles. Pursed lip breathing may be evident.

The Medical Research Council (MRC) 'dyspnoea scale' is a useful assessment tool. It provides a measure of the impact of COPD, and, combined with spirometry, it can help in assessing its severity.

Table 4.1

MRC dyspnoea scale

MRC dyspnoea scale

Grade 1: I only get breathless with strenuous exercise.

Grade 2: I get short of breath when hurrying on the level or up a slight hill.

Grade 3: I walk slower than other people of the same age when walking at my own pace on the level.

Grade 4: I stop for breath after walking every 100 yards or after a few minutes on the level.

Grade 5: I am too breathless to leave the house or breathless when dressing or undressing.

(NICE, 2004)

The 'six minute walking test' is also a useful measure of how far a patient can walk in a specified time. The test is completed indoors on the level and the patient can stop as often as they need to. Serial tests over years can be a useful aid to assess disease progression and can help assess the effectiveness of interventions.

Visual analogue scales can also be used to establish how breathless a patient feels. Typically, a 10 cm line is labelled 'not breathless at all' at one end and 'extremely short of breath' at the other. Patients mark the line to indicate how breathless they feel. Clearly this is subjective and there is a risk that it will lack reproducibility, but visual analogue scales may nevertheless help assess deterioration associated with disease progression and may help establish the effectiveness of interventions.

In practice, it is often more useful to ask questions such as 'Can you walk up the stairs?' or 'Can you walk from the surgery to the pharmacy?'

Patients in whom a diagnosis of COPD is considered should also be asked about the presence of the following factors: weight loss, effort intolerance, waking at night, ankle swelling, fatigue, occupational hazards, chest pain and haemoptysis. The last two symptoms are uncommon in COPD and raise the possibility of alternative diagnoses. Weight loss and ankle swelling are discussed in Chapters 9 and 10.

A full blood count will identify anaemia or polycythemia and body mass index should be calculated. Pulse oximetry can be used to assess the need for oxygen therapy. See Chapter 10 for further discussion of this.

Differential diagnosis

Patients with COPD may have other disorders, and differential diagnosis should include a consideration of bronchiectasis, congestive cardiac failure and carcinoma of the bronchus. Patients should have a chest X-ray to help exclude other pathologies.

Asthma and COPD

Asthma and COPD

One of the most common areas for confusion is differentiating between asthma and COPD. This is because they are both obstructive disorders, and they have similar signs and symptoms. It is important to differentiate correctly between asthma and COPD because this has implications for pharmacological and other aspects of management. One should be fairly certain of diagnosis before informing a patient that they have a progressive irreversible disorder.

History-taking is the key to differentiating between asthma and COPD and differential diagnosis on the basis of clinical history can be accurate (Fabbri *et al.*, 2003), although respiratory investigations, such as challenge tests and assessment of domiciliary peak flow variation, can add important information where the diagnosis is uncertain. Questions should focus on smoking, family history, previous respiratory symptoms, childhood illnesses, atopic features and variability. Day-to-day variability is associated with asthma, as are night-time symptoms.

One of the most useful ways of differentiating COPD from asthma is to ask about the patterns and onset of breathlessness. Breathlessness in asthma may be linked to trigger factors such as pollen or dust, whereas breathlessness in COPD is likely to occur during exercise, for instance when climbing stairs, and it is also likely to be gradually progressive, increasing in severity each year. The MRC dyspnoea scale (see table 4.1) may be useful in this respect. Careful questioning may provide evidence of progressive deterioration in MRC score, which is a feature of COPD, unlike most asthma.

Table 4.2 lists other factors which may help differentiate between asthma and COPD (NICE, 2004).

Table 4.2

Differential diagnosis between asthma and COPD

	COPD	Asthma
Smoker or ex-smoker	*Nearly all*	*Possibly*
Symptoms under age 35	*Rare*	*Often*
Chronic productive cough	*Common*	*Uncommon*
Breathlessness	*Persistent and progressive*	*Variable*
Night-time waking with breathlessness and/or wheeze	*Uncommon*	*Common*
Significant diurnal or day-to-day variability of symptoms	*Uncommon*	*Common*

If COPD is suspected, the diagnosis should be supported or confirmed with spirometry. Examination and history-taking in isolation may be misleading and there is a danger that the patient may have a different disorder, or COPD combined with another disorder. Once COPD is confirmed, spirometry should be performed at least annually.

Spirometry

Spirometry (from the Latin word 'spiro' meaning breathe) is the measurement of breathing. It is an accurate, objective and reproducible measurement of lung volume and airflow.

NICE (2004) states that spirometry is the only accurate method of measuring airflow obstruction in patients with COPD and is fundamental to making the diagnosis. It is important to remember, however, that this must be in addition to a thorough clinical history and examination and should be performed when the patient is clinically well. If performed when the patient has a respiratory infection or during an exacerbation results may be misleading.

Spirometry is a relatively risk free procedure, however it requires effort by the patient and this results in an increase in intra-thoracic, intra-abdominal and intra-ocular pressures. The list below outlines the cautions to consider prior to spirometry and it would be appropriate to seek medical advice before performing spirometry on patients with:

- haemoptysis
- pneumothorax, within eight weeks
- unstable cardiovascular state, e.g. recent myocardial infarction, uncontrolled hypertension, uncontrolled angina, pulmonary embolism

- recent eye surgery
- recent thoracic or abdominal surgery
- thoracic, cerebral or abdominal aneurysm.

(ARTP, 2006)

As patients with COPD may have advanced damage which has occurred prior to presentation of symptoms, many patients demonstrate a significant decline in lung function at their first assessment. This may come as a shock to patients and information giving should be handled sensitively.

Differing types of spirometry equipment are currently used which allow the measurement of dynamic lung volumes. These can be conveniently divided into two categories.

Volume-displacing spirometers

These are designed to measure exhaled volumes of air. Examples include wedge bellows, rolling seal and water-filled spirometers. As the individual exhales into the equipment, volume changes in the spirometer reflect equal and opposite changes in the lung volumes. The advantages of these machines are their precision and ease of operation. Disadvantages include lack of portability and that they are capable of measuring an expiratory manoeuvre only.

Flow-sensing spirometers

These machines are more common in primary care. Their advantages include that they are portable, they measure inspiratory as well as expiratory manoeuvres, they will calculate predicted values for individual patients and they will provide a printout of the results. The printout includes graphical displays of the manoeuvre and all values and recordings.

One example of a flow-sensing spirometer is the 'turbine' spirometer. Airflow in a turbine spirometer causes a vane in the flow head to rotate. The rotating vane interrupts a light source and the number of rotations can be measured and a flow signal generated.

Another example is a 'pneumotachograph' spirometer. A pneumotachograph spirometer contains a manometer which detects the fall in pressure across an obstruction in a tube. As the patient blows into the tube the pressure before the obstruction is greater than that beyond and volume and flow of air is calculated from the pressure difference.

ATPS/BTPS

Lung volumes should be measured at the temperature and pressure conditions of the lungs, that is, body temperature and pressure saturated with water vapour (BTPS). All spirometers measure gas volumes at the temperature and pressure in the recording equipment, that is ambient temperature and pressure saturated with water vapour (ATPS). This has implications for the reliability of measurement of lung volumes because the volume of air changes as it changes temperature and so the volume of air inside the lungs may change when it is exhaled.

Most spirometry equipment has in-built mechanisms for converting the gas volumes from ATPS to BTPS, although some equipment needs adjusting when room temperature changes. It is important that you understand the manufacturer's instructions.

Care and maintenance of spirometry equipment

Care and maintenance of spirometry equipment is essential for accurate and reliable measurements. It is also important that the equipment is cleaned at the end of each spirometry session. The manufacturer's instructions must also be followed in order to fulfill the requirements of the warranty.

In order to reduce the risk of bacterial cross infection, mouthpieces with filters are used to provide a barrier between the patient and the equipment. Disposable mouthpieces are most commonly used and these should be discarded after each single patient use.

The calibration check is a most important part of a quality control procedure. This must be performed on a daily basis or before each spirometry session in order to determine the accuracy and precision of the spirometry equipment. A one-litre or three-litre calibration syringe is used to check the calibration. The known volume of air is injected into the spirometer at differing flow rates and calibration results should be recorded in the spirometer or documented manually in a log book. A volume accuracy within three per cent or 50 ml is acceptable. If inaccuracies are detected the spirometer should be calibrated, or, if this is not possible, it should be removed from service and the manufacturer should be contacted.

'Normal' values

Following spirometric testing it is standard practice to compare the measured values to predicted normal values which are derived from population studies (see 'Interpretation of spirometry data' below). These studies provide a calculation of the average reference values and range for an individual. These are based on various factors which influence normal lung volumes.

>**Age:** Lung volume decreases with age from 25 years. Predicted values are therefore lower as age increases.
>**Gender:** Males have larger lung volumes than females and the differences emerge during puberty.
>**Height:** Increased lung volumes are seen with increased height.
>**Ethnicity:** Variables exist between ethnic groups. For example, Asian groups have relatively small lungs in relation to their body size.

Whilst predicted values are useful, it is important to remember that they are not completely reliable and that a patient's normal lung volumes may differ from the predicted for their age, height, race and sex, even if there is no abnormality.

What is being measured?

Vital capacity (VC) is the maximum amount of air that is exhaled from the lungs following maximal inhalation. Vital capacity may be measured in two ways: slow vital capacity and forced vital capacity.

Slow vital capacity (SVC), also referred to as relaxed vital capacity (RVC), measures the volume of air which is slowly exhaled from the lungs following maximal inspiration. SVC is measured and expressed in litres and is not time dependent. When performing this test, the individual is instructed to inhale fully, seal the lips around the mouthpiece and to slowly and steadily breathe out through the tube until no more air can be exhaled. Nose clips should be worn for the SVC procedure to prevent escape of air through the nasal passages.

Forced vital capacity (FVC) is the volume of air that is exhaled from the lungs following full inspiration during a forced manoeuvre. A forced manoeuvre involves the patient breathing out as quickly as they can. The FVC manoeuvre therefore measures the volume of air and how quickly air is exhaled from the lungs. When performing this test the individual is required to breathe in fully as in the VC manoeuvre, but, unlike the VC procedure, they are required to forcibly and rapidly expel the air from the lungs and to continue blowing out for as long as possible. Results from spirometry can be displayed in a number of ways, but one of the most useful methods of displaying results is graphically on a volume time curve (Figure 4.1).

Figure 4.1

Volume time curve demonstrating a normal pattern

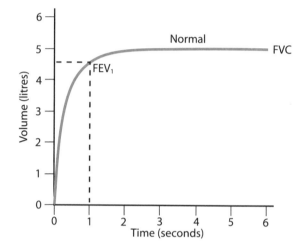

As the individual begins to exhale rapidly during the FVC manoeuvre, the graph rises sharply upwards and then curves smoothly and convexly as the flow of air reduces. The graph flattens as the exhalation continues until all air is exhaled from the lungs. FVC can be read directly from the graph.

The volume time curve can give other useful information. Perhaps the most useful reading is the FEV_1. This is the volume of air expired in the first second of the FVC manoeuvre.

If an individual has an obstructive disorder it will take them longer to exhale during the FVC manoeuvre, and, while the FVC may not be affected, the FEV_1 will certainly be reduced. It is useful to express the FEV_1 as a percentage of the FVC (or SVC whichever is greater). This FEV_1/VC ratio is sometimes referred to as the forced expiratory ratio or FEV_1 per cent. This ratio defines the presence or absence of obstruction in the airways. In healthy lungs, a forced expiration will result in at least 75 per cent of the air being exhaled in the first second of a FVC manoeuvre. Ratios vary with age, but, as a rule of thumb, a ratio of less than 70 per cent is deemed to indicate obstructive lung disease (NICE, 2004) because it takes longer to exhale the air through an obstructed airway.

Figure 4.2

Volume time curve demonstrating an obstructive pattern compared to a normal curve

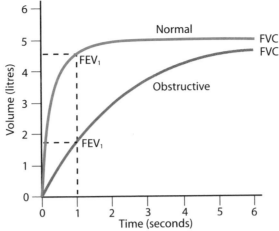

Figure 4.2 shows a typical trace of an obstructive pattern. This presents as a reduced FEV_1. Clearly the ratio of the FEV_1 to FVC is also reduced, demonstrating airflow obstruction. It can be seen that there is also a small reduction in FVC, often seen in obstructive lung diseases, which can be a result of the collapse of small airways during the forced manoeuvre causing air trapping. It is, therefore, necessary to perform an SVC first to obtain accurate readings of lung volume. Patients with more severe COPD may have a more significantly reduced FVC.

Figure 4.3

Volume time curve demonstrating a restrictive pattern compared to a normal curve

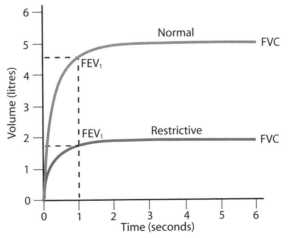

Spirometry will also detect restrictive lung diseases, as shown by Figure 4.3. Restrictive diseases and disorders prevent full expansion of the lungs and may be due to changes in the chest wall, lung tissue and pleura. It is important to note that unlike obstructive disorders, restrictive lung disorders will not necessarily reduce the diameter of airways, and the shape of the curve is therefore similar to a 'normal' curve.

The reduction in lung volume caused by restrictive disorders will mean that the FVC and FEV_1 are reduced compared to normal. The forced expiratory ratio, however, will be normal (above 70 per cent) or high. This is because, although the vital capacity is low, the airflow is not reduced because the size of the airways remains normal. Therefore it is important to calculate the FEV_1/FVC ratio when diagnosing an obstructive disorder and not rely on an FEV_1 measurement.

Interpretation of spirometry data

A step-wise, systematic approach to interpretation is recommended. This will ensure that spirometry results are reviewed correctly for each individual.

It is vital to ensure accuracy and reproducibility prior to interpretation of results. The competence of the technician is paramount. One normal-looking trace is not sufficient; there must be a minimum of three technically-acceptable recordings. The tracings should be forced from the start of the test and should demonstrate a curve that is smooth and convex and free from irregularities that may, for example, be caused by coughing during the forced manoeuvre.

The curve should rise steeply upwards and plateau for at least two seconds. This plateau may take up to 15 seconds to reach for a person with COPD and sufficient time must be allowed to ensure the individual has exhaled completely.

Reproducibility is demonstrated by comparing each FVC attempt. At least two readings should be within 100 ml and five per cent of each other. A maximum of eight attempts is recommended, however many patients will demonstrate progressively worsening results due to fatigue.

Step 1: Is obstruction present?

This is established from the FEV_1/FVC ratio, which is less than 70 per cent in obstructive lung diseases such as COPD. If the ratio is greater than 70 per cent, no obstruction has been demonstrated and the individual may not have COPD.

The calculation for this ratio is as follows:

$$\frac{\text{Measured } FEV_1 \times 100}{\text{Measured FVC}}$$

Step 2: What is the level of FVC and FEV$_1$?

Predicted values for the patient are first calculated, based [...] age, gender and ethnicity. Modern, electronic spiromet[...] this automatically from the patient data. Measured values [...] compared to the predicted values and expressed as a perc[...]

According to NICE (2004) guidelines, a normal FVC is defined as being greater than 80 per cent of the predicted value. In obstructive patterns in the early stages of COPD there will be little, if any, effect on the forced vital capacity because obstruction does not prevent the lungs from holding normal volumes of air. However, in more severe disease a reduction may be seen due to airway collapse and air trapping.

If the FVC is low, that is less than 80 per cent of the predicted value, this indicates small lung volumes which may be due to a restrictive lung disease. If detected, this would indicate the need for further investigation and usually hospital referral which will allow access to more detailed investigation of lung function. Prior to referral, ensure that the test has been performed correctly. Errors in technique may result in a false restrictive reading. For example, a patient who does not inhale or exhale completely would produce a low vital capacity reading.

The calculation for percentage of predicted FVC is:

$$\frac{\text{Measured FVC} \times 100}{\text{Predicted FVC}}$$

Once it has been established that a patient has an obstructive curve, defined as an FEV$_1$/FVC ratio below 70 per cent, FEV$_1$ can be compared to predicted values in order to calculate the severity of COPD. A normal FEV$_1$ is defined as being greater than 80 per cent of the predicted value (NICE, 2004), although some guidelines suggest that a patient with such a percentage can still have COPD if their FEV$_1$/FVC ratio is reduced (GOLD, 2006).

The calculation for percentage of predicted FEV$_1$ is:

$$\frac{\text{Measured FEV}_1 \times 100}{\text{Predicted FEV}_1}$$

For patients with COPD, the severity of the disease is determined by comparing the FEV$_1$ to the predicted value. Varying guidelines for the diagnosis and classification of COPD exist. The NICE classification (2004) is outlined in Table 4.3.

Table 4.3

*Classification of
severity of COPD
(NICE, 2004)*

Mild COPD	$FEV_1 = 50$ to 80%
Moderate COPD	$FEV_1 = 30$ to 49%
Severe COPD	$FEV_1 < 30\%$

Reversibility testing

Reversibility testing

In the past, a measurement of the degree of reversibility, using bronchodilators or corticosteroids, has been used to differentially diagnose asthma and COPD. There are a number of difficulties with using reversibility testing and reliance on it can lead to an incorrect diagnosis. One problem is that there is considerable variability in the change of FEV_1 response to the same stimulus from day to day, making reversibility testing unreliable (Calverley *et al.*, 2004). A large response, in excess of 400 ml, is suggestive of an asthmatic component but a minority of COPD patients may have a response greater than 400 ml and some asthma patients may demonstrate very little reversibility. In most cases, the diagnosis of COPD is suggested by the combination of the clinical history and baseline spirometry and reversibility testing may not add any additional information.

It may be that symptoms are disproportionate to the spirometric impairment. Patients may have chronic bronchitis and emphysema but this may not necessarily be fully reflected in spirometric readings. In circumstances such as these, further investigations may be appropriate. Other investigations might include transfer factor of the lung for carbon monoxide (TLCO) and CT scan of the thorax (NICE, 2004)

References

Association for Respiratory Technology and Physiology (ARTP) (2006). *Spirometry Handbook,* 2nd edn. Birmingham: ARTP.

Calverley, P.M.A., Burge, P.S., Spencer, S., Anderson, J.A. and Jones, P.W. (2004). Bronchodilator reversibility testing in chronic obstructive pulmonary disease. *Thorax*, 58, 659–664.

Fabbri, L.M., Romagnoli, M., Corbetta, L., Casoni, G., Busljetic, K. and Turato, G. (2003). Differences in airway inflammation in patients with fixed airway obstruction due to asthma or chronic obstructive pulmonary disease. *Journal of Respiratory Care Medicine*, 167(2), 418–424.

Global Initiative for Chronic Obstructive Lung Disease (GOLD) (2006) *Global Strategy for the Diagnosis, Management and Prevention of Chronic Obstructive Pulmonary Disease*. Workshop Report November 2006. Bethesda: NLHBI/WHO.

National Institute for Health and Clinical Excellence (NICE) (2004). Chronic Obstructive Pulmonary Disease: National clinical guideline on management of chronic obstructive pulmonary disease in adults in primary and secondary care. *Thorax*, 59 (Suppl. 1), 1–232.

Chapter 5
Pharmacological management of chronic disease
Jenny Sparrow

The use of drug therapy in COPD can lead to substantial symptomatic relief and reduction in complications. Ideally it would also slow the underlying disease progression, slowing the decline in lung function and reducing mortality, but whether or not any current therapies achieve this is not yet fully established.

Central to most patients' pharmaceutical management are bronchodilators.

Bronchodilators

Bronchodilators

In COPD, unlike asthma, the majority of airways obstruction is, by definition, irreversible. It is perhaps unsurprising, then, that inhaled bronchodilators do not have as marked a beneficial effect on lung function as in asthmatic patients. Changes in lung function, however, do not always correlate well to improvements in exercise capacity and reduction of breathlessness in individual patients (Hay et al., 1992) and bronchodilators do appear to support both of these. These benefits are thought to be due to the correction of any reversible element of the patient's bronchoconstriction and the reduction of over-inflation (Belman et al., 1996). From more recent trials, in long-acting inhaled bronchodilators particularly, benefits have become apparent in other patient-centred outcomes such as health status and reduction in exacerbations. Bronchodilators therefore remain the mainstay of therapy in COPD.

There are three separate therapeutic categories of bronchodilators to be considered, each with different potential benefits and adverse effects:
- inhaled beta$_2$-agonists
- inhaled anti-muscarinics
- oral xanthine derivatives.

Inhaled beta$_2$-agonists

Inhaled beta$_2$-agonists

There are two groups:

- short-acting agents – e.g. salbutamol and terbutaline
- long-acting agents – e.g. salmeterol and formoterol.

Beta-agonists (beta-adrenergic agonists) mimic the effects of noradrenaline on beta receptors, part of the sympathetic nervous system. Modern drugs are selective for beta$_2$ receptors, which are found on the smooth muscle cells surrounding the bronchi and bronchioles. When activated by noradrenaline or beta-agonists, beta$_2$ receptors stimulate the enzyme adenylate cyclase causing increased production of cyclic adenosine monophosphate (cAMP) which leads to relaxation of the smooth muscle, resulting in bronchodilation. Beta receptors are also found in other tissues, including the heart, although these are of the beta$_1$ subtype.

Selective beta$_2$-agonists may cause an increase in heart rate (which may cause palpitations). Other systemic side effects include fine tremor, nervous tension, headache and muscle cramps. Hypokalaemia may result from higher doses. Side effects are mostly dose related and are more common with nebulised therapy and longer-acting agents than with short-acting agents administered by hand-held inhalers. Reducing the dose or switching nebulised salbutamol to a hand-held inhaler usually reduces or stops side effects. Oral salbutamol is still available but side effects are more troublesome and it is rarely used since the development of effective inhaled bronchodilators.

Short-acting beta$_2$-agonists (SABA)

SABA start to work within five minutes and effects last for four to six hours. This makes them ideal for 'when required' use by the mildly-affected patient, who may experience problems only on exertion. SABA are usually first choice treatment for patients with newly-diagnosed COPD. Benefits shown in trials include improvements in breathlessness and lung function (Cook et al., 2001).

Patients with moderate to severe disease may prefer to use them regularly, e.g. two to four times daily, to help keep symptoms under control, but extra doses may still be taken on a 'when required' basis. Patients who remain symptomatic despite use of SABA, or who find they need to take their SABA frequently, should be offered further bronchodilator treatment. SABA appear to remain effective as a 'when required' bronchodilator even when other bronchodilators are being taken regularly (Cook *et al.*, 2001), so a patient's SABA should be continued alongside other bronchodilators.

SABA may also be taken in anticipation of breathlessness, for example, taking a dose prior to physical exertion to prevent or reduce the breathlessness. For mildly-affected patients this may be only for fairly strenuous exercise, whereas for those with more severe disease it may be necessary to help them climb the stairs or carry out daily activities such as washing and dressing.

In the UK, these inhalers are usually blue (for dry-powder inhalers part of the device may be a different colour) and are often referred to as 'reliever inhalers', as they relieve symptoms of breathlessness and wheezing. Patients should be told to keep their SABA ('blue reliever inhaler') close at hand at all times in case it is needed. It may be useful to have more than one, allowing storage in different places (e.g. one upstairs, one downstairs) and ensuring that when one inhaler runs out another is always available.

Long-acting beta-agonists (LABA)

LABA have a duration of action of at least 12 hours. Salmeterol has a slower onset of action than SABA, taking 10 to 20 minutes, while formoterol starts to act as quickly as SABA, within five minutes. Benefits of regular, twice-daily use of LABA in COPD include improvements in symptoms, lung function and a reduction in the number of exacerbations and hospitalisations (Shukla *et al.*, 2006). These inhalers are usually green (although part of the device may be a different colour). Most patients will be used to using a SABA inhaler only when they need it and experiencing a rapid effect, so it is important to explain that effects may not be as immediately obvious after each dose. The main benefits of LABA are obtained from regular use at a fixed dose and frequency (twice daily). Patients should continue to use their SABA as a 'when needed' ('reliever') inhaler.

Inhaled anti-muscarinics (anticholinergics)

Inhaled anti-muscarinics

The parasympathetic nervous system, mediated by the transmitter acetylcholine, is responsible for the resting tone of the bronchial smooth muscle. In COPD this resting tone is increased, resulting in bronchoconstriction. Anti-muscarinic bronchodilators block the acetylcholine (i.e. cholinergic) receptors and are frequently referred to as anticholinergics. However, they act specifically at the muscarinic type of cholinergic receptors so 'anti-muscarinic' (or muscarinic antagonist) is a more accurate term. Like beta$_2$-agonists, there are both short-acting and long-acting drugs.

Anti-muscarinic receptors are found in many other tissues, e.g. heart, eye, exocrine glands, gut, bladder and ureters, but use of the inhaled route minimises the amount of drug reaching the systemic circulation and thus systemic side effects. The most common side effect is dry mouth, since muscarinic receptors are involved in secretion of saliva. In the long term this may be associated with dental caries. Other bodily secretions are also reduced, including respiratory. As with beta-agonists, side effects are more common with nebulised high doses and with the long-acting drug than for low doses of short-acting drug delivered by hand-held inhaler.

Anti-muscarinic drugs may increase intra-ocular pressure so should be used with caution in patients with glaucoma, particularly when used in combination with beta-agonists. Acute angle closure glaucoma has been reported. For this reason, nebulised ipratropium should be given using a mouthpiece rather than a mask for patients with glaucoma, or any patient on long-term nebulised therapy, to protect the eyes, and patients should be warned to avoid getting any powder or spray from inhalers in their eyes.

Other rarer side effects include urinary retention and constipation (so caution is advised in prostatic hyperplasia and bladder outflow obstruction) and, with tiotropium, arrhythmias such as atrial fibrillation and possibly urinary tract infections.

Short-acting anti-muscarinics

Ipratropium is the only agent now available in the UK and is an alternative to SABA as first choice agent in COPD. It is slightly more effective than SABA in terms of improving lung function and health status and reducing the need for oral corticosteroids (Appleton et al., 2006). The onset of action of ipratropium is slower than SABA (30 to 60 minutes), so it is less suitable than SABA for 'when needed' use. A single dose lasts up to six hours and it is usually prescribed up to four times daily. Patients should be warned that it does not work as quickly as SABA. Some use it regularly, four times daily, every day, while others may vary the frequency day to day depending on their symptoms.

Long-acting anti-muscarinics

Tiotropium is a once-daily long-acting anti-muscarinic licensed for the treatment of COPD. Its mode of action differs from previous inhaled anti-muscarinics, in that it is selective for certain subtypes of muscarinic receptors. M_1 receptors are found in the parasympathetic nerves in the airway where they facilitate cholinergic transmission. M_3 receptors are found in the bronchial smooth muscle and mediate bronchoconstriction. Blockade of M_1 or M_3 receptors therefore leads to bronchodilation. M_2 receptors, on the other hand, are involved in a negative feedback loop. Stimulation of the M_2 receptor causes a reduction in the release of acetylcholine from the nerves, so blocking this receptor may actually reduce the anti-muscarinic effects by preventing this inhibition. Although tiotropium binds to and blocks all three of these receptor subtypes, it is very slow to dissociate from M_1 and M_3 receptors, leading to sustained bronchodilation. However, its dissociation from M_2 receptors is much more rapid, so the unwanted effect of blocking this receptor is not prolonged.

Clinical trials have confirmed that the effects of tiotropium last at least 24 hours, allowing once-daily dosing (Littner et al., 2000). It is usually taken in the morning but may be taken at a different time of day if the patient prefers. As with LABA, it is important to explain that benefits are not felt as quickly as with short-acting bronchodilators, and regular use of a fixed daily dose gives the best results. A meta-analysis of trials showed reduced exacerbations, reduced symptoms and improved health status compared to placebo and ipratropium through a hand-held inhaler (Barr et al., 2006). Tiotropium also reduced COPD-related hospitalisations compared to placebo. It appeared to slow the decline in FEV_1 and there was a non-statistically significant reduction in pulmonary mortality. Further trials are needed to investigate these possible effects.

Unlike beta-agonists, the concurrent use of short-acting and long-acting anti-muscarinic drugs is not recommended. Ipratropium also blocks M_1, M_2 and M_3 receptors, but it dissociates from all three subtypes relatively quickly (hence its shorter duration of action). Theoretically its effect on M_2 receptors could reduce the effect of tiotropium.

If tiotropium is started then ipratropium should be stopped. There is no comparative data on tiotropium and nebulised ipratropium in acute or chronic settings. If a patient on tiotropium is admitted to hospital and prescribed nebulised ipratropium, then tiotropium should be withheld.

Xanthine derivatives

Xanthine derivatives

Xanthines (also called methylxanthines) such as theophylline and caffeine are naturally occurring substances in plants. Theophylline and caffeine are found in tea, and caffeine in coffee, chocolate and cola drinks. Their mode of action is not entirely understood. They inhibit phosphodiesterase, an enzyme which breaks down cAMP (cyclic adenosine monophosphate). This raises the levels of cAMP, which leads to bronchodilation by relaxation of the bronchial smooth muscle. There is also evidence for effects of theophylline on diaphragmatic strength, mucociliary clearance and increasing cardiac output. Aminophylline and theophylline are usually given as a sustained release preparation to allow twice-daily dosing (although once-daily dosing may be used if symptoms are particularly troublesome during the day or night only). Theophylline has been used for many years in COPD but the advent of safer alternatives has relegated it to third choice therapy in recent years. It improves lung function and arterial blood gas tensions but its effect on exercise performance is less clear, and patients prefer it to placebo (Ram *et al.*, 2002). However, its value in COPD patients is limited by various factors.

- It has a narrow therapeutic range – that is, the toxic dose is only a little higher than the effective one.
- It is metabolised by a cytochrome P450 enzyme in the liver, and thus has many drug interactions and other factors (e.g. smoking status, heart failure) which affect its metabolism. For an individual patient, it can therefore be difficult to predict the optimal dose, especially in the elderly. To ensure a therapeutic dose for a particular patient, the serum level must be checked and the dose adjusted accordingly.
- Side effects are not uncommon and toxic levels can cause fatal effects (see Table 5.1).

Table 5.1

Side effects of theophylline

At therapeutic or toxic serum levels	Nausea and/or vomiting
	Dyspepsia
	Tachycardia/palpitations
	Tremor
	Insomnia
	Headache
	Hypokalaemia
At toxic levels	Arrhythmias
	Seizures
	Fatalities

Although side effects may occur even at therapeutic serum levels, the presence of side effects should prompt a check of the serum level to ensure that it is not toxic. A trough level of 10 to 20 mg/l is generally considered the therapeutic range. Most side effects of theophylline are dose related, so, if they are troublesome and the level is towards the higher end of the therapeutic range, a reduction in dosage may help. Note that when toxic levels occur, the severe side effects may not be preceded by 'warning signs' in the form of less serious side effects such as nausea.

Smoking causes induction (an increase in quantity) of the liver enzymes which metabolise theophylline, so smokers generally require a higher dose than non-smokers. Following smoking cessation, this effect wears off over several months, so serum levels should be closely monitored during this time and the dose reduced as necessary.

Because of these issues, national guidelines recommend that theophylline be reserved for those cases in whom short-acting and long-acting inhaled bronchodilators have already been tried or for patients unable to use inhaled therapy (NCCCC, 2004). If used, plasma levels need to be monitored. Reassessment should be made when interacting medication is added. For example if macrolide (e.g. erythromycin) or quinolone (e.g. ciprofloxacin) antibiotics are prescribed for lower respiratory tract infections, the dose of theophylline may need to be temporarily reduced.

There may be differences in bioavailability between different brands of theophylline or aminophylline sustained release products, so these should always be prescribed by brand to ensure continuity of treatment. Common brands include Uniphyllin Continus, Slo-Phyllin, Nuelin SA (theophylline sustained release) and Phyllocontin Continus (aminophylline sustained release).

Corticosteroids

Corticosteroids (often referred to as 'steroids') are found naturally in the body and these low physiological levels have many effects essential in the response to stress and injury and in regulating the metabolism of protein, carbohydrate and fat. Larger pharmacological doses also have useful immunosuppressant and anti-inflammatory effects but their many other, usually unwanted, effects can result in serious side effects.

Inhaled corticosteroids

Inhaled corticosteroids

Inhaled corticosteroids (ICS) have been the gold standard treatment in asthma for many years. Inflammation in COPD, however, is of a different nature. The effects and role in therapy of ICS in COPD are less clear and have been the subject of much research and discussion in recent years. There has been speculation that they may slow the decline in lung function in COPD and reduce mortality, but this is still controversial.

Four major long-term trials of ICS in COPD (Burge *et al.*, 2000; Pauwels *et al.*, 1999; LHJRG, 2000; Vestbo *et al.*, 1999) designed to examine the effect of ICS on FEV_1 decline, showed no slowing in the rate of decline in patients treated with ICS. Of two meta-analyses combining trials which measured decline in FEV_1, one showed no effect of ICS on FEV_1 decline (Highland *et al.*, 2003) while the other showed a small effect, particularly with high dose regimens (Sutherland *et al.*, 2003).

However, treatment with ICS does reduce the number of exacerbations and slows the rate of decline in health status (Burge *et al.*, 2000; Calverley *et al.*, 2003; Sin *et al.*, 2003). The effect on exacerbation rate is more marked in patients with moderate to severe airflow obstruction (Jones *et al.*, 2003). Observational studies using general practice databases suggest that ICS may reduce mortality (Sin & Tu, 2001), but this has not been shown in a prospective randomised controlled trial.

One such trial designed specifically to examine effects on mortality of ICS, LABA and combination, showed that fluticasone monotherapy did not reduce all-cause mortality compared to placebo (Calverley *et al.*, 2007). A pooled analysis of seven ICS trials in COPD showed a small reduction in mortality in patients with FEV_1 less than 60 per cent predicted (Sin *et al.*, 2005). The research and debate continues. Many recent trials have studied the effects of combined LABA and ICS rather than ICS alone and these are discussed below.

Current national and international guidelines recommend inhaled steroids for patients with moderate to severe disease (FEV_1 less than 50 per cent predicted) who have repeated exacerbations (i.e. two or more in a year) requiring treatment with antibiotics and/or oral corticosteroids (NICE, 2004; GOLD, 2006). There is probably no role for this treatment in patients with mild disease. Oral corticosteroid reversibility tests do not predict response to inhaled corticosteroids and should not be used to identify which patients should be prescribed inhaled corticosteroids (Burge *et al.*, 2003; NICE, 2004).

None of the inhalers containing corticosteroid alone are licensed for use in the treatment of COPD in the UK and this should be borne in mind when prescribing. Trials have used a variety of different corticosteroids of different potencies, including triamcinolone, budesonide and fluticasone, with various doses and devices. The optimum dose is not yet established, but there is no evidence to support doses greater than fluticasone 1 mg daily.

Local side effects to inhaled steroids can occur, particularly with higher doses. Oral candidiasis (thrush) can occur due to local immunosuppression and hoarse voice due to weakening of the vocal cord muscles by drug deposited there during inhalation. These effects can be reduced by using a large volume spacer for metered dose inhalers and by rinsing the mouth out after use of ICS.

ICS pose far less risk of systemic side effects than oral steroids. The incidence and clinical significance of many potential or reported systemic side effects in adults is controversial, with varying results from different trials, and longer trials are needed. Side effects reported in trials include skin bruising and striae (purple marks) and reduced bone marrow density (Pauwels *et al.*,

1999; Scanlon *et al.*, 2004) but the effect on fracture rate is not clear. There are also reports of glaucoma and cataracts (Cumming *et al.*, 1997). There is some evidence of effect on biochemical markers of adrenal function but the clinical significance of this is unclear. An increased incidence of pneumonia has occurred in patients given high dose fluticasone (Kardos *et al.*, 2007; Calverley *et al.*, 2007).

These risks should be discussed with the patient but put into context against the expected benefits in terms of symptom control, improved health status, reduced risk of exacerbations (potentially allowing less exposure to oral steroids) and other possible benefits. The British National Formulary (www.bnf.org, accessed 1.8.07) recommends that a 'steroid card' be issued to all patients on high dose inhaled steroids.

The lack of an obvious and rapid effect of ICS may reduce compliance with regular dosing. Patients should be made aware that, unlike bronchodilators, benefits of ICS are not apparent after individual doses. It is essential to use ICS regularly (e.g. twice daily) as a 'preventer' inhaler, to help manage COPD symptoms and reduce exacerbations in the long term. Extra doses should not be taken 'when required' for breathlessness.

Combination treatment with ICS and long-acting bronchodilators

Combination treatment

Both long-acting inhaled bronchodilators and inhaled corticosteroids have been shown to reduce exacerbations, raising the question of whether or not combination treatment with a drug from each class has any additive benefit over treatment with one class alone. Trials formally assessing the additive benefits of ICS with tiotropium are lacking (although some trials of tiotropium allowed patients to continue ICS, so, for the proportion of patients in the tiotropium arm who also happened to be on ICS, any effect of tiotropium was additive (Casaburi *et al.*, 2002; Vincken *et al.*, 2002)).

However, there are two combination products available containing a LABA with ICS: formoterol with budesonide, and salmeterol with fluticasone. Combination treatment has benefits over monotherapy in terms of symptom control, reduction in exacerbations and improvement in health status (Szafranski *et al.*, 2003; Kardos *et al.*, 2007; Calverley *et al.*, 2007). One prospective study designed to examine effect on mortality found a reduction that did not quite reach statistical significance in all-cause mortality with combined fluticasone and salmeterol compared to placebo (Calverley *et al.*, 2007). Larger trials are needed to clarify this issue.

Oral corticosteroids

Oral cortico-steroids

Short courses of oral corticosteroids (usually prednisolone) are used to good effect for acute exacerbations of COPD, with few short-term side effects, and patients may ask why they cannot continue to take them. The most serious limitation of oral steroid therapy is the risk of long-term side-effects. This risk is higher with higher doses, long courses or long-term maintenance therapy or frequent short courses. There is little evidence for benefits and oral steroids are therefore not recommended as maintenance treatment in the NICE guideline (NICE, 2004).

Some long-term side effects of oral steroids

- Blunted immune response: increased susceptibility and severity of infections
- Osteoporosis
- Adrenal suppression
- Peptic ulceration
- Muscle wasting and tendon rupture
- Fluid retention
- Hyperglycaemia and diabetes
- Weight gain and redistribution of body fat
- Skin atrophy and impaired healing

However, the NICE guideline recognises that some patients with advanced COPD may require maintenance oral corticosteroids when these cannot be withdrawn following an exacerbation. If this is the case, the dose should be kept as low as possible and monitoring for osteoporosis and/or prophylactic medication is recommended. Current national guidelines on corticosteroid-induced osteoporosis recommend that all patients over 65 years who will be on any dose of oral corticosteroids for more than three months should be started on prophylactic medication, usually a bisphosphonate (e.g. alendronate, risedronate, etidronate) with calcium and vitamin D supplementation. Younger patients should be educated on general lifestyle measures to reduce risk (e.g. regular weight-bearing exercise, good nutrition especially with calcium and vitamin D, not smoking and so on) and a bone scan undertaken to assess risk and need for prophylactic treatment (Bone and Tooth Society *et al.*, 2002).

Patients should be given a steroid card, made aware of potential side effects and advised to take the daily dose as a single dose each morning after breakfast. Treatment should not be stopped suddenly (except after short courses of up to about three weeks) and an increase in dose may be required during periods of illness.

Immunisation

Immunisation

The Department of Health has recommended since 1993 that immunisation against influenza should be given to at-risk populations, including those with chronic pulmonary disease. A reduction in influenza mortality and hospitalisation has been demonstrated following the use of influenza vaccination in the elderly population with chronic lung disease (Nichol *et al.*, 1999a). Evidence specific to COPD is limited and some trials used vaccines other than those used today. However, it appears that inactivated influenza vaccine reduces exacerbations in COPD patients and there is no evidence of an increase in exacerbations in the weeks immediately following vaccination (Poole *et al.*, 2006).

Vaccination of elderly persons with chronic lung disease against pneumococcus, and against both pneumococcus and influenza, have been shown to reduce hospitalisations for pneumonia and influenza and risk of death from all causes (Nichol *et al*, 1999b; Nichol, 1999). Influenza vaccine is adjusted each year to provide protection against the most appropriate strain of influenza. All patients with COPD should be offered influenza vaccine, with readministration annually, and pneumococcal vaccine, with readministration every five years. Both may be given at the same time provided separate sites are used (Salisbury *et al.*, 2006).

Pharmacological management of chronic disease

Mucolytic agents

Mucolytic agents

Mucolytic agents reduce sputum viscosity in vitro and are therefore intended to facilitate expectoration. N-acetylcysteine also has antioxidant activity which may contribute to its effects. The group includes:

- carbocisteine tablets (Mucodyne)
- mecysteine tablets (previously called methyl cysteine; Visclair)
- N-acetylcysteine (not available in oral form in the UK but used widely in other parts of Europe for various indications).

Despite widespread use in Europe, mucolytic therapy was 'blacklisted' in the NHS and therefore unable to be prescribed until 2003. Systematic reviews suggest that mucolytics can reduce exacerbations in patients with chronic bronchitis and COPD (Poole & Black, 2006). NICE therefore recommend mucolytic therapy be considered in patients with a chronic cough productive of sputum to try and improve symptoms and reduce exacerbations (NICE, 2004). After a four-week trial the patient should be reviewed. If there is no apparent benefit, the mucolytic should be stopped. If, however, there seems to be symptomatic improvement, such as a reduction in cough and sputum, then the mucolytic should be continued at a lower maintenance dose.

Nebulised dornase alfa (DNase) reduces sputum viscosity by breaking down DNA found in sputum and is useful in cystic fibrosis. Studies in COPD have been disappointing, however, so it is not licensed for use in COPD patients.

Symptomatic control – which bronchodilator?

Symptomatic control

A short-acting bronchodilator (beta$_2$-agonist or anti-muscarinic) used 'when required' is recommended as initial therapy in the NICE guideline (2004). If one does not control symptoms adequately the other can be substituted or the two can be used together, usually regularly up to four times daily. In practice, a beta$_2$-agonist (e.g. salbutamol) is usually the first of the two to be prescribed. A combination product is available containing both salbutamol and ipratropium, which may be more convenient for patients who use both drugs regularly. Patients using this regularly are often also prescribed a separate salbutamol inhaler for 'when required' use.

Although all the bronchodilators act mainly by relaxing the smooth muscle around the airways, each class achieves this by a different pathway. Some drugs (e.g. theophylline) may also have other beneficial actions. This provides a rationale for prescribing them in combination for patients where one alone is insufficient to control symptoms. Clinical trials have shown that a combination of drugs from different classes is more effective than monotherapy. Bronchodilator combinations with evidence of increased benefit include:

- beta$_2$-agonist and short-acting anti-muscarinics
- beta$_2$-agonist and theophylline
- anti-muscarinics and theophylline.

If patients are still symptomatic despite a combination of short-acting bronchodilators, then a long-acting bronchodilator should be tried. This may be a LABA or long-acting anti-muscarinic. Combination treatment with a LABA and ICS in moderate to severe disease reduces symptoms of breathlessness and this may be tried if a long-acting bronchodilator alone does not control symptoms (Mahler et al., 2002).

Theophylline is generally reserved for patients for whom long-acting bronchodilators are insufficient or who are unable to use inhaled drugs.

There is limited data regarding additive benefits of combination therapy with a LABA and tiotropium, although short-term trials show additive effects in terms of lung function and rescue inhaler use, with treatment well tolerated (Van Noord et al., 2005). The benefits and optimal place in therapy of this regimen are not yet fully established.

The clinical effectiveness of treatments can be assessed by improvements in symptoms, activities of daily living, exercise capacity and lung function. When prescribed to control day-to-day symptoms such as breathlessness and exercise limitation, therapy should be reviewed regularly and individual drugs stopped after a suitable trial period (e.g. four weeks) if they appear to be ineffective. Such discontinuation would be inappropriate, however, for drugs also prescribed to reduce exacerbations, such as long-acting bronchodilators.

Reducing exacerbations

Exacerbations of COPD, as well as being significant events in themselves, have been shown to have marked consequences for patients. Patients suffering more exacerbations have significantly worse health status (Seemungal et al., 2000) and show a more rapid decline in lung function (Donaldson et al., 2002). Exacerbations may also cause primary physician consultations and hospitalisations and often involve extra treatment with antibiotics, oral corticosteroids and possibly other medication which may cause short- or long-term side effects. Thus there are many potential direct and indirect benefits to be gained if exacerbations can be prevented or reduced.

The following pharmacological measures have been shown to reduce exacerbations and should be considered for individuals with frequent exacerbations:

- vaccinations (recommended for all patients with COPD)
- long-acting bronchodilators
- inhaled steroids (the effect is more marked in patients with moderate to severe disease)
- LABA and ICS combined
- mucolytics.

It may be helpful to think in terms of secondary prevention measures. Drugs such as aspirin, beta-blockers and statins are routinely prescribed (unless contraindicated) to patients post-myocardial infarction to reduce the risk of further events. In the same way, many of the therapies listed above should be routinely considered for those suffering frequent exacerbations of COPD, to reduce the risk of further exacerbations.

For patients exacerbating frequently, it is particularly important to check inhaler technique, assess compliance as far as possible and ensure that the patient understands their disease and treatments as well as possible. Patients should be educated about the signs and symptoms of exacerbations and encouraged to present to a healthcare professional sooner rather than later when an exacerbation occurs. For some patients it may be useful to provide 'rescue courses' of corticosteroids and/or antibiotics to keep at home, allowing a prompt start to treatment if signs of respiratory infection or exacerbation of COPD occur. Medical attention should then be sought as soon as possible.

Trials to date of long-term prophylactic antibiotics to reduce COPD exacerbations have many methodological limitations and UK guidelines do not recommend their use (NICE, 2004).

Treatment of cor pulmonale

Treatment of cor pulmonale

Patients with cor pulmonale should be assessed for long-term oxygen therapy (LTOT, see Chapter 7). The peripheral oedema associated with cor pulmonale is generally treated with diuretics, although there is no specific evidence base for their use in COPD. Other drugs are not recommended in the current NICE (2004) guideline. Trials of nifedipine and digoxin for cor pulmonale have not shown any benefit in patients without left ventricular failure and there are limited studies on angiotensin converting enzyme inhibitors and angiotension receptor antagonists.

Managing anxiety and depression

Anxiety and depression

Anxiety and depression may simply co-exist with COPD or develop as a consequence of the progressive symptoms of COPD and their impact on patients' lives. Those with severe COPD are more at risk (Van Manen *et al.*, 2002). Clinicians should be alert to the presence of anxiety and depression in COPD patients, particularly in patients with more severe symptoms and limitations. There is limited trial data for pharmacological treatment of anxiety and depression in COPD patients and standard pharmacotherapy should be prescribed where necessary.

Drug delivery systems in COPD

Drug delivery systems

The objective of inhaled therapy in COPD is to maximise the quantity of drug that reaches its site of action, while minimising side effects from unintended systemic absorption. The most critical element in determining this balance is drug particle size.

- Particles of between two and five microns penetrate best into the medium-sized and small bronchioles, where they can influence bronchoconstriction.

- Particles smaller than this will tend to penetrate deeper into the alveoli, where they can be absorbed into the circulation.
- Particles larger than 15 microns will remain in the upper airways and exert no beneficial effects.

Most inhalers are designed to deliver particles of between 0.5 and 10 microns, with the majority being at the optimum five micron size. Unfortunately, however, poor inhaler technique tends to mean that a relatively small proportion of the drug actually reaches its site of action.

Good inhaler technique is vital in COPD. The standard metered dose inhaler (MDI or 'press-and-breathe' inhaler) without a spacer is rarely appropriate for elderly patients. Alternative approaches include the use of a spacer, breath-actuated aerosol inhalers and dry-powder devices. For more severely affected patients, nebulised therapy is often considered. Although this is generally thought of as the most effective delivery system, there is, in fact, no clear evidence in older patients to support the view that nebulisers are any better than other devices, when properly used (Poundsford, 1997).

Metered dose inhalers (MDIs)

Metered dose inhalers

Many formulations must be shaken well before use. The patient should remove the protective mouthpiece, breathe out, then seal their mouth around the mouthpiece and press the canister to release the spray of drug at the same time as starting a slow deep inhalation. They should then hold their breath for as long as is comfortable before expiring. For a second actuation, this whole process should be repeated.

MDIs are available for most inhaled drugs and for many drugs they are the cheapest option. However, co-ordination between pressing the canister and breathing in may be difficult. If the canister is fired before or after inhalation rather than during, most or all of the drug will simply be deposited in the mouth and oropharynx or blown into the air. Most MDIs do not have a dose counter so it can be hard to tell when the canister is empty. For patients with arthritic hands, pressing the canister down may be difficult. A Haleraid is available to fit over certain MDIs, allowing the patient to squeeze their fingers and thumb together easily to fire the canister making it much more manageable for many people.

Breath-actuated aerosols

Breath-actuated aerosols

Easi-Breathe and Autohaler are examples of breath-actuated aerosols. After shaking, these are each primed for use in different ways: either pulling down the mouthpiece cover or pushing up a lever. Then the patient simply has to breathe out, seal their mouth round the mouthpiece, take a slow deep inhalation and hold their breath. The device is pressurised and will release a dose automatically on inhalation. To take a second actuation, the inhaler must be 'reset' and primed again. These devices may be simpler to use than MDIs and remove the need to co-ordinate pressing and breathing. However, they are only available for a limited range of drugs.

Dry-powder inhalers

Dry-powder inhalers (DPIs)

Various dry-powder inhalers are available. All have different methods for preparing a dose for inhalation. Some have separate capsules which must be placed into an inhaler and pierced. After priming the device, the patient should breathe out away from the mouthpiece, seal their mouth around the mouthpiece, take a rapid deep inhalation and hold their breath as long as comfortable. Unlike aerosol inhalers, dry-powder inhalers are fully reliant on the patient's inspiratory flow to transport the drug (as powder) from inside the inhaler down into the airways. As such, most require a greater inspiratory flow than aerosol inhalers and this may be particularly difficult for elderly COPD patients. Most DPIs have dose counters allowing easy identification of the number of doses left. Ease of use varies between devices. Many DPIs are unique to one drug, although both the Accuhaler and Turbohaler have a range of drugs from different classes. Patients with arthritis may find it difficult to manipulate these devices to prepare a dose.

Spacers

Spacers

Spacers (holding chambers) remove the need for co-ordination between pressing and breathing in when using MDIs. They are designed to ensure maximum lung deposition of a suitable particle size to reach the lower airways. Adding a large volume spacer also improves both acquisition and retention of technique, reduces systemic absorption of inhaled corticosteroids and improves lung deposition. Therefore the first choice recommendation for inhaled therapy in COPD within the NICE guideline (2004) is a hand-held device with a spacer. Large volume spacers are also useful for giving higher doses in an emergency. Repeated actuations of SABA from an MDI inhaled via a large volume spacer is an alternative to nebulised SABA.

There are two main ways of using spacers. The MDI should be shaken (where necessary), the mouthpiece cap removed and the MDI mouthpiece fitted into the spacer. The patient should seal their mouth round the other end of the spacer, before firing a single actuation into the spacer. At the same time or shortly after the actuation, a single slow deep inhalation should be taken and the breath held as long as is comfortable. Alternatively, for patients who find it difficult to take and hold a deep breath, 'tidal breathing' method may be used (with spacers containing two way valves). After firing the canister, several normal breaths in and out are taken, keeping the mouth sealed around the spacer throughout.

For both methods, the process should be repeated from the start to take a second actuation. Multiple actuations should never be released into the spacer at the same time.

Cleaning instructions should be given. Spacers should be washed once a month with warm water and detergent (e.g. washing up liquid), rinsed and then allowed to drip dry as wiping them with a cloth or towel can cause static charges inside and therefore affect drug deposition. It is essential to explain to the patient the benefits of using a spacer, and reinforce this regularly, as many patients own spacers and have previously agreed to use them but do not use them regularly. Spacers should be replaced every six to twelve months.

Large volume spacers such as Volumatic and Nebuhaler are better established, with more evidence than smaller spacers, but, by definition, are bulky. Many patients prefer medium or small volume spacers, particularly for use when out of the house. Not all MDIs fit all spacers so compatibility must be checked before prescribing.

Other issues regarding inhaler devices and spacers

Other issues

- In terms of devices, what a patient can use and will use may be completely different, particularly with spacers. It is essential to consider both.

- The best device for use at home may not be appropriate for a reliever inhaler that needs to be taken out and used in public. For non-housebound patients, ensure that they have a reliever device that they are comfortable with carrying and using (usually not a large volume spacer).
- Check expiry dates when reviewing a patient's inhalers. Out-of-date devices may indicate low use, i.e. poor compliance, or may result from having more than one of the same inhaler and using the newer one first.
- For each patient, it is best to keep the number of different devices to a minimum to reduce the number of different techniques the patient must become expert in and reduce potential for confusion between techniques.
- Generic prescribing of inhaled drugs and devices can lead to difficulties, e.g. 'salbutamol breath-actuated aerosol' may mean Easi-breathe or Autohaler, which look very different and are primed for use in different ways. Different manufacturers also produce MDIs with different-shaped mouthpieces which fit different spacer devices. It is important to speak to the patient to establish exactly which device they normally use and check compatibility with spacers where necessary.
- Ensure the patient knows how to clean their inhaler or mouthpiece and how to tell when each device is empty. When reviewing a patient's inhalers, always check that they are not empty.
- Most inhalers require 'priming' before first use or after a period of not being used – e.g., for MDIs, spraying one or more doses into the air. Check the manufacturer's instructions for each device.
- With some devices (e.g. MDI alone, some DPIs), the patient may feel or taste the medication in their mouth and throat, while other devices generally leave no taste or feel (e.g. MDI with spacer, other DPIs). Some patients prefer the taste or feel as a reassurance that they have received a dose and may take some convincing that this is not necessary (e.g. if switched to MDI with spacer). Others dislike this sensation and prefer devices without it.

Pharmacological management of chronic disease

Table 5.2

Common inhalers available in the UK and doses used in COPD
(NB Not all products listed are licensed for use in COPD.)

Drug name (generic)	Common UK brand names	Some available devices in the UK	Usual dose for COPD	Usual colour of device
SHORT-ACTING BETA-AGONISTS				
Salbutamol (NB This is called albuterol in the US.)	Ventolin Salamol Airomir Asmasal	MDI Breath-actuated aerosol (Easi-breathe, Autohaler) DPIs (Accuhaler, Clickhaler, Cyclohaler, Easyhaler, Pulvinal)	200 micrograms (100–400 micrograms) prn or regularly qds and prn (NB Not all devices are licensed for COPD.)	Blue or white with blue
		Nebuliser solution	2.5 mg or 5 mg qds and/or prn	
Terbutaline	Bricanyl	DPI (Turbohaler)	500 micrograms prn or regularly	White with blue
		Nebuliser solution	5–10 mg qds and/or prn	
LONG-ACTING BETA-AGONISTS				
Formoterol	Oxis, Atimos Foradil	MDI DPIs (eg Turbohaler)	12 micrograms bd (may be expressed as dose leaving mouthpiece: 9–10 micrograms is equivalent to 12 micrograms, depending on device)	White with green
Salmeterol	Serevent	MDI DPI (Accuhaler)	50 micrograms bd	Green
SHORT-ACTING ANTI-MUSCARINIC				
Ipratropium	Atrovent Respontin	MDI DPI (Aerohaler)	40 micrograms qds	White, clear and green
		Nebuliser solution	250–500 micrograms qds prn	
LONG-ACTING ANTI-MUSCARINIC				
Tiotropium	Spiriva	DPI (Handihaler)	18 micrograms od (usually morning)	Grey with green capsules

CORTICOSTEROIDS				
Beclometasone	Becotide Becloforte Beclazone Qvar Clenil	MDI Breath-actuated aerosol (Easi-breathe, Autohaler) DPIs (Clickhaler, Pulvinal, Cyclohaler)	Limited evidence in COPD and dose unclear. (NB For Qvar, half the dose is clinically equivalent to other beclometasone.)	Brown or maroon
Budesonide	Pulmicort	MDI DPI (Accuhaler, Easyhaler, Novolizer)	400 micrograms bd used in most recent COPD trials. (NB Not licensed alone for COPD.)	Brown or white with brown
		Nebuliser solution	Not recommended for use in COPD.	
Ciclesonide	Alvesco	MDI	Not currently used in COPD.	Orange
Fluticasone	Flixotide	MDI DPI (Accuhaler)	500 micrograms bd used in most recent COPD trials. (Not licensed alone for COPD.)	Orange
		Nebuliser solution	Not recommended for use in COPD.	
Mometasone	Asmanex	DPI (Twisthaler)	Not currently used in COPD.	White with maroon
COMBINATION SABA and short-acting anti-muscaric				
Salbutamol & ipratropium	Combivent	MDI	100 + 20 micrograms/puff 2 puffs bd qds	Grey with white, orange and green
		Nebuliser solution	2.5 mg/500 micrograms up to qds	
COMBINATION LABA and ICS				
Salmeterol & fluticasone	Seretide	MDI DPI (Accuhaler)	Licensed dose for COPD 500 + 50 micrograms bd	Purple
Formoterol & budesonide	Symbicort	DPI (Turbohaler)	Licensed dose for COPD 400 + 12 micrograms bd	White with red

Pharmacological management of chronic disease

Nebulisers

Nebulisers

The aim of treatment with nebulisers is to deliver a therapeutic dose of drug as an aerosol in the form of respirable particles within a fairly short period of time, usually five to ten minutes (Nebuliser Project Group of the BTS, 1997). The main uses in COPD are for:

- short-term use during more severe acute exacerbations
- patients who experience distressing or disabling breathlessness despite maximal therapy. If nebuliser therapy is prescribed, the patient should be provided with equipment, servicing, advice and support. Adequate assessment and confirmation of improvement must be established before continuing therapy and the recommendations provided by the British Thoracic Society (Nebuliser Project Group of the BTS, 1997) can be used.

A choice between facemask and mouthpiece should be offered unless the drug specified requires a mouthpiece (e.g. anti-muscarinic).

The type of nebuliser recommended for home use consists of a compressor or pump, a nebuliser chamber and a mask or mouthpiece. Air is blown by the compressor into the chamber, where it is forced through a drug solution and past a series of baffles. The solution is converted into a fine mist of respirable particles which is then inhaled by the patient through the mask or mouthpiece (see Figure 5.1).

Figure 5.1

The mechanics of the nebuliser delivery system

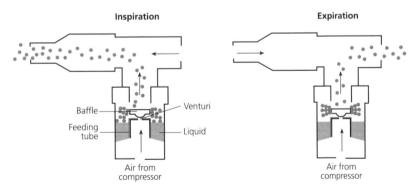

The size of particles produced is determined by:

- the characteristics of the nebuliser chamber
- the output speed of the compressed gas
- drug viscosity
- usual fill volume (minimum 2.5 ml, maximum varies but often 5 ml – check the manufacturer's instructions).

Provided all these are well matched, and the compressor serviced regularly, consistent particle size can be achieved. If there is a mismatch between chamber and compressor type, or a drug is used in the wrong type of chamber, delivery effectiveness may be dramatically reduced.

It is important that patients are aware how to set up and use their nebuliser and compressor properly, how to clean it, when to change the various parts and how and when to get it serviced.

In the hospital environment, piped oxygen may be used to drive nebulisers. This is not recommended in COPD due to the risk of hypercapnia. If oxygen therapy is needed it should be administered simultaneously via a nasal cannulae. The driving gas for the therapy should always be specified in the prescription.

Patients on nebulised bronchodilators at home should still be prescribed other inhalers as usual, including short-acting bronchodilator inhalers. These may be used instead of the nebuliser for some doses, or used on a 'when required' basis between nebulised doses or when going out.

Compliance with therapy

Compliance with therapy

Control of any chronic disease depends on two factors. First, that patients are prescribed the correct therapy, and, second, that they are able and willing to take it correctly. In COPD, where patients are often on multiple therapies using unfamiliar devices, the potential for inadequate control is huge.

Long-term compliance

Long-term compliance in COPD is generally poor, with only about 50 per cent of patients taking their therapy correctly and on a regular basis (James *et al.*, 1985). Even those who think they are using inhaled therapy as prescribed are unlikely to be receiving optimum doses: studies have suggested that fewer than 25 per cent of patients are likely to be using metered dose inhalers accurately (Larsen *et al.*, 1994).

This situation is not inevitable. Even in older patients, who might be expected to have more difficulties, inhaler technique can be satisfactorily taught, provided factors such as hand strength and dementia are taken into account (Gray *et al.*, 1996). Where this proves difficult, the use of inhaler aids or other devices may be advantageous. Equally, the appropriate use of fixed combination therapies may assist compliance.

Measures to maximise compliance in COPD

- Keep numbers of different therapies used to a minimum. Combination inhalers may be helpful in this respect.
- Ensure that the patient understands the purpose of each drug, when to take it and expected effects.
- Avoid complex regimens where possible.
- Choose inhaler devices that the patient is physically capable of using and feels comfortable with.
- Ensure that adequate tuition in inhaler technique is given.
- Check inhaler technique on every visit and retrain if necessary.
- Ask about side effects or problems.

Future developments

Future developments

Theophylline is a non-specific phosphodiesterase (PDE) inhibitor. Two oral selective PDE_4 inhibitors, cilomilast and roflumilast, are undergoing clinical trials currently, which may offer benefits without the many side effects that can occur with theophylline. Alternative long-acting anti-muscarinic drugs are also in formulation. Trials investigating the benefits of combining existing therapies are underway, and others hoping to show the efficacy of once-daily inhaled steroids and long-acting beta-agonists. In a completely different approach to therapy, agents designed to stimulate the immune system are also under investigation.

Key points

- Currently available drug treatments for COPD improve symptom control, reduce exacerbations and slow the decline in health status. Questions and controversy remain over their effects on the decline in lung function and on mortality. More research is needed to clarify these issues.
- Although most of the airways obstruction in COPD is irreversible, many patients still derive symptomatic improvement from bronchodilators.

Management of COPD in primary and secondary care

- Combinations of anti-muscarinics and beta-agonists may improve symptom control.
- Long-acting beta-agonists and anti-muscarinics may be helpful in patients who are still symptomatic despite frequent doses of short-acting bronchodilators.
- Theophylline is limited by side effects and risk of toxicity. It should be used only in selected patients under supervision.
- Inhaled steroids should be considered in patients with FEV_1 less than 50 per cent predicted who have two or more exacerbations per year.
- Immunisation against influenza and pneumococcus should be offered to every patient with COPD.
- Nebulisers deliver bronchodilator therapy within five to ten minutes and are used primarily in treating acute exacerbations not responding to inhaled therapy.
- Home nebuliser therapy is controversial and should be initiated only following expert assessment.
- Patient education in the use of inhalers and nebulisers is essential.
- Many patients use inhalers incorrectly and fail to keep to dosage regimens. Check inhaler technique and usage frequently.

References

Appleton, S., Jones, T., Poole, P., Pilotto, L., Adams, R., Lasserson, T.J., Smith, B. and Muhammad, J. (2006). Ipratropium bromide versus short-acting beta$_2$ agonists for stable chronic obstructive pulmonary disease. (Cochrane Review). *The Cochrane Library*, 2.

Barr, R.G., Bourbeau, J., Camargo, C.A. and Ram, F.S.F. (2006). Tiotropium for stable Chronic Obstructive Pulmonary Disease: A meta analysis. *Thorax*, 61, 854–862.

Belman, M.J., Botnick, W.C. and Shin, J.W. (1996). Inhaled bronchodilators reduce dynamic hyperinflation during exercise in patients with chronic obstructive pulmonary disease. *American Journal of Respiratory and Critical Care Medicine*, 153, 967–975.

Bone and Tooth Society, National Osteoporosis Society and Royal College of Physicians (2002). *Glucocorticoid-induced Osteoporosis: Guidelines for prevention and treatment*. London: RCP.

Burge, P.S., Calverley, P.M.A., Jones, P.W., Spencer, S., Anderson, J.A. and Maslen, T.K. (2000). Randomised, double-blind, placebo-controlled study of fluticasone propionate in patients with moderate to severe Chronic Obstructive Pulmonary Disease: The ISOLDE trial. *British Medical Journal*, 320, 1297–1303.

Burge, P.S., Calverley, P.M.A., Jones, P.W., Spencer, S. and Anderson, P.A. (2003). Prednisolone response in patients with Chronic Obstructive Pulmonary Disease: Results from the ISOLDE trial. *Thorax*, 58, 654–658.

Calverley, P.M.A., Pauwels, R., Vestbo, J., Jones, P., Pride, N., Gulsvik, A., Anderson, J. and Maden, C.; Trial of Inhaled Steroids and Long-acting Beta$_2$-agonists Study Group. (2003). Combined salmeterol and fluticasone in the treatment of Chronic Obstructive Pulmonary Disease: A randomised controlled trial. *Lancet*, 361, 449–456.

Calverley, P.M.A., Anderson, J.A., Celli, B., Ferguson, G.T., Jenkins, C., Jones, P.W., Yates, J.C. and Vestbo, J.; TORCH investigators. (2007). Salmeterol and fluticasone propionate and survival in chronic obstructive pulmonary disease. *New England Journal of Medicine*, 356, 775–789.

Casaburi, R., Mahler, D.A., Jones, P.W., Wanner, A., San Pedro, G., ZuWallack, R.L., Menjoge, S.S., Serby, C.W. and Witek Jr, T. (2002) A long-term evaluation of once-daily inhaled tiotropium in chronic obstructive pulmonary disease. *European Respiratory Journal*, 19, 217–224.

Cook, D., Guyatt, G., Wong, E., Goldstein, R., Bedard, M., Austin, P., Ramsdale, H., Jaeschke, R. and Sears, M. (2001). Regular versus as-needed-short-acting inhaled beta-agonist therapy for chronic obstructive pulmonary disease. *American Journal of Respiratory and Critical Care Medicine*, 163, 85–90.

Cumming, R.G., Mitchell, P. and Leeder, S.R. (1997). Use of inhaled corticosteroids and the risk of cataracts. *New England Journal of Medicine*, 337, 8–14.

Donaldson, G.C., Seemungal, T.A., Bhowmik, A., Jeffries, D.J. and Wedzicha, J.A. (2002). Relationship between exacerbation frequency and lung function decline in chronic obstructive pulmonary disease. *Thorax*, 57, 847–852.

Global Initiative for Chronic Obstructive Lung Disease (GOLD) (2006) *Global Strategy for the Diagnosis, Management and Prevention of Chronic Obstructive Pulmonary Disease*. Workshop Report November 2006. Bethesda: NLHBI/WHO.

Gray, S.L., Williams, D.M., Pulliam, C.C., Sirgo, M.A., Bishop, A.L. and Donohue, J.F. (1996). Characteristics predicting incorrect metered-dose inhaler technique in older subjects. *Archives of Internal Medicine*, 156, 984–988.

Hay, J.G., Stone, P., Carter, J., Church, S., Eyre-Brook, A., Pearson, M.G., Woodcock, A.A. and Calverley, P.M. (1992). Bronchodilator reversibility, exercise performance and breathlessness in stable chronic obstructive pulmonary disease. *European Respiratory Journal*, 5, 659–664.

Highland, K.B., Strange, C. and Heffner, J.E. (2003). Long-term effects of inhaled corticosteroids on FEV_1 in patients with Chronic Obstructive Pulmonary Disease: A meta analysis. *Annals of Internal Medicine*, 138, 969–973.

James, P.N., Anderson, J.B., Prior, J.G., White, J.P., Henry, J.A. and Cochrane, G.M. (1985) Patterns of drug taking in patients with chronic airflow obstruction. *Postgraduate Medical Journal*, 61, 7–10.

Jones, P.W., Willits, L.R., Burge, P.S. and Calverley, P.M. (2003). Disease severity and the effect of fluticasone propionate on chronic obstructive pulmonary disease exacerbations. *European Respiratory Journal*, 21, 68–73.

Kardos, P., Wencker, M., Glaab, T. and Vogelmeier, C. (2007). Impact of salmeterol/fluticasone versus salmeterol on exacerbations in severe chronic obstructive pulmonary disease. *American Journal of Respiratory and Critical Care Medicine*, 175, 144–149.

Larsen, J.S., Hahn, M., Ekholm, B. and Wick, K.A. (1994). Evaluation of conventional press-and-breathe metered-dose inhaler technique in 501 patients. *Journal of Asthma*, 31, 193–199.

Littner, M.R., Ilowite, J.S., Tashkin, D.P., Friedman, F., Serby, C.W., Menjoge, S.S. and Witek, T.J. (2000). Long-acting bronchodilation with once-daily dosing of tiotropium (Spiriva) in stable chronic obstructive pulmonary disease. *American Journal of Respiratory and Critical Care Medicine*, 161, 1136–1142.

Lung Health Study Research Group (2000). Effect of inhaled triamcinolone on the decline in pulmonary function in chronic obstructive pulmonary disease. *New England Journal of Medicine*, 343, 1902–1909.

Mahler, D.A., Wire, P., Horstman, D., Chang, C-N., Yates, J., Fischer, T. and Shah, T. (2002). Effectiveness of fluticasone propionate and salmeterol combination delivered via the Diskus device in the treatment of chronic obstructive pulmonary disease. *American Journal of Respiratory and Critical Care Medicine*, 166, 1084–1091.

Van Manen, J.G., Bindels, P.J., Dekker, F.W., Ijzermans, C.J., van der Zee, J.S. and Schade, E. (2002). Risk of depression in patients with chronic obstructive pulmonary disease and its determinants. *Thorax*, 57, 412–416.

Pharmacological management of chronic disease

National Collaborating Centre for Chronic Conditions (NCCCC) (2004). Chronic Obstructive Pulmonary Disease: National clinical guideline on management of chronic obstructive pulmonary disease in adults in primary and secondary care. *Thorax*, 59 (Suppl. 1), 1–232.

Nebuliser Project Group of the British Thoracic Society (BTS) (1997). Current best practice for nebuliser treatment. *Thorax*, 52 (Suppl. 2), S1–S24.

Nichol, K.L. (1999). The additive benefits of influenza and pneumococcal vaccinations during influenza seasons among elderly persons with chronic lung disease. *Vaccine*, 17 (Suppl. 1), S91–S93.

Nichol, K.L., Baken, L. and Nelson, A. (1999a). Relation between influenza vaccination and outpatient visits, hospitalization, and mortality in elderly persons with chronic lung disease. *Annals of Internal Medicine*, 130, 397–403.

Nichol, K.L., Baken, L., Wuorenma, J. and Nelson, A. (1999b). The health and economic benefits associated with pneumococcal vaccination of elderly persons with chronic lung disease. *Archives of Internal Medicine*, 159, 2437–2742.

Van Noord, J.A., Aumann, J.L., Janssens, E., Smeets, J.J., Verhaert, J., Disse, B., Mueller, A. and Cornelissen, P.J. (2005). Comparison of tiotropium once daily, formoterol twice daily and both combined once daily in patients with COPD. *European Respiratory Journal*, 26, 190–191.

Pauwels, R.A., Löfdahl, C.G., Laitinen, L.A., Schouten, J.P., Postma, D.S., Pride, N.B., and Ohlsson, S.V. (1999). Long-term treatment with inhaled budesonide in persons with mild chronic obstructive pulmonary disease who continue smoking. *New England Journal of Medicine*, 340, 1948–1953.

Poole, P.J. and Black, P.N. (2006). Mucolytic agents for chronic bronchitis or chronic obstructive pulmonary disease. (Cochrane Review), *The Cochrane Library*, 3.

Poole, P.J., Chacko, E., Wood-Baker, R.W.B. and Cates, C.J. (2006). Influenza vaccine for patients with chronic obstructive pulmonary disease. (Cochrane Review), *The Cochrane Library*, 1.

Pounsford, J.C. (1997). Nebulisers for the elderly. *Thorax*, 52 (Suppl. 2), S53–S55.

Ram, F.S.F., Jones, P.W., Castro, A.A., de Brito Jardim, J.R., Atallah, A.N., Lacasse, Y., Mazzini, R., Goldstein, R. and Cendon, S. (2002). Oral theophylline for chronic obstructive pulmonary disease. (Cochrane Review), *The Cochrane Library*, 3.

Salisbury, D., Ramsay, M. and Noackes, K. (2006). *Immunisation against Infective Disease*. London: DH.

Scanlon, P.D., Connett, J.E., Wise, Tashkin, D.P., Madhok, T., Skeans, M., Carpenter, P.C., Bailey, W.C., Buist, A.S., Eichenhorn, M., Kanner, R.E., Weinmann, G.; the Lung Health Study Research Group. (2004). Loss of bone density with inhaled triamcinolone in Lung Health Study II. *American Journal of Respiratory and Critical Care Medicine*, 170, 1302–1309.

Seemungal, T.A.R., Donaldson, G.C., Paul, E.A., Bestall, J.C., Jeffries, D.J. and Wedzicha, J.A. (2000). Effect of exacerbation on quality of life in patients with chronic obstructive pulmonary disease. *American Journal of Respiratory and Critical Care Medicine*, 161, 1608–1613.

Shukla, V.K., Chen, S., Boucher, M., Mensinkai, S. and Dales, R. (2006). Long-acting Beta$_2$-agonists for the Maintenance Treatment of Chronic Obstructive Pulmonary Disease with Reversible and Non-reversible Airflow Obstruction: A systematic review of clinical effectiveness. Technology Report 65. Ottawa: Canadian Co-ordinating Office for Health Technology Assessment.

Sin, D.D. and Tu, J.V. (2001). Inhaled corticosteroids and the risk of mortality and morbidity in elderly patients with chronic obstructive pulmonary disease. *American Journal of Respiratory and Critical Care Medicine*, 164, 580–584.

Sin, D.D., McAlister, F.A., Man, P. and Anthonisen, N.R. (2003). Contemporary management of Chronic Obstructive Pulmonary Disease: Scientific review. *Journal of the American Medical Association*, 290, 2301–2312.

Sin, D.D., Wu, L., Anderson, J.A., Anthonisen, N.R., Buist, A.S., Burge, P.S., Calverley, P.M., Connett, J.E., Lindmark, B., Pauwels, R.A., Postma, D.S., Soriano, J.B., Szafranski, W. and Vestbo, J. (2005). Inhaled corticosteroids and mortality in chronic obstructive pulmonary disease. *Thorax*, 60, 992–997.

Sutherland, E.R., Allmers, H., Ayas, N.T., Venn, A.J. and Martin, R.J. (2003). Inhaled corticosteroids reduce the progression of airflow limitation in Chronic Obstructive Pulmonary Disease: A meta analysis. *Thorax*, 58, 937–941.

Szafranski, W., Cukier, A., Ramirez, A., Menga, G., Sansores, R., Nahabedian, S., Peterson, S. and Olsson, H. (2003). Efficacy and safety of budesonide/formoterol in the management of chronic obstructive pulmonary disease. *European Respiratory Journal*, 21, 74–81.

Vestbo, J., Sørenson, T., Lange, P., Brix, A., Torre, P. and Viskum, K. (1999). Long-term effect of inhaled budesonide in mild and moderate Chronic Obstructive Pulmonary Disease: A randomised controlled trial. *Lancet*, 353, 1819–1823.

Vincken, W., van Noord, J.A., Greefhorst, A.J.M., Bantje, T.A., Kesten, S., Korducki, L. and Cornelissen, P.J.G. (2002). Improved health outcomes in patients with COPD during one year's treatment with tiotropium. *European Respiratory Journal*, 19, 209–216.

Chapter 6
Managing an exacerbation in primary care
Pat Fairclough

Exacerbations are serious events for patients with COPD; not only are the episodes themselves distressing, debilitating and even devastating, but they are linked to increased morbidity and mortality (Seemungal et al., 1998). They result in absence from work and inability to carry out usual activities and so the loss of a normal everyday life. Recovery can take many weeks and in some cases health can be impaired for months. More severe exacerbations may necessitate a hospital admission and can eventually lead to death.

In addition, the frequency of exacerbations may accelerate reduction of lung function (Donaldson, et al., 2002) which in turn increases the severity of COPD. Exacerbations may occur at any stage on the disease trajectory but are most common in severe patients (Donaldson & Wedzicha, 2006). As the COPD becomes more severe so do the exacerbation symptoms and recuperation takes longer (Wedzicha & Donaldson, 2003). The majority of exacerbations are managed in primary care with many being dealt with by patients themselves without the assistance of health professionals (Seemungal et al., 1998). The numbers of exacerbations are indefinite as many are not reported. Primary care records underestimate the true figure of exacerbations (MacNee, 2003).

In most instances, patients with exacerbations of COPD can be managed in their own homes but hospital admission will be necessary for some patients needing increased levels of treatment. It is vital that exacerbations are well managed in the community to prevent patients having unnecessary hospital admissions and to reduce morbidity. This chapter will consider the community management of exacerbations which includes recognition, assessment, treatment and prevention.

Management of COPD in primary and secondary care

Definition

Definition

There is debate about the definition of an exacerbation of COPD. NICE (2004) proposes that an exacerbation is a sustained worsening of a patient's symptoms from the patient's usual stable state that is beyond normal day-to-day variations and is acute in onset. Common symptoms are worsening breathlessness, coughing, increased sputum production and change in sputum colour. The change in these symptoms often requires a change in medication.

A precise classification is difficult due to the nature of COPD; day-to-day fluctuations in symptoms and lung function are part and parcel of the normal course of the disease. The importance of symptoms and their variability are subjective and patients can fail to appreciate them. Seemungal *et al.* (1998) estimate that 50 per cent of symptomatically-defined exacerbations are unreported as patients are accustomed to day-to-day symptom changes. The pattern of exacerbations varies from one patient to another and also from one exacerbation to another in the same patient (Scott *et al.*, 2006).

Defining exacerbations by the medical intervention needed is also problematic as these will vary according to the individual patient circumstances, the services available and the treatment practices in each area. Exacerbations of the same severity may require hospital admission in one district but be managed by a 'Hospital at Home' scheme in another. Rodriguez-Roisin (2000) proposed staging COPD exacerbations based on the level of healthcare needed; mild can be managed by the patient at home, moderate needed some medical assistance and severe required hospitalisation.

Causes

Causes

There are a range of factors which contribute to exacerbations; these may be respiratory infections or non-infective causes. Over half have been attributed to upper respiratory tract infections predominately Rhinovirus, the common cold virus (Wedzicha, 2004). Other viruses known to cause exacerbations are influenza, parainfluenza, Coronavirus, Picornavirus, Adenovirus and respiratory syncytial virus (Greenberg *et al.*, 2000).

Managing an exacerbation in primary care

Bacterial causes for infection include *Haemophilus influenzae, Streptococcus pneumoniae, Moxarella catarrhalis, Chlamydia pneumoniae, Haemophilus parainfluenzae* and *Pseudomonas aeruginosa* (Sapey & Stockley, 2006). Stable COPD patients have a high prevalence of lower airway bacterial colonisation, up to 40 per cent, which is associated with disease severity and smoking (Zalacain *et al.*, 1999). This colonisation is related to the characteristics and frequency of exacerbations (Patel *et al.*, 2002).

Non-infective agents such as common pollutants are also linked with exacerbations. These include nitrogen dioxide, particulates, sulphur dioxide and ozone (Wedzicha, 2002). Changes in the weather and temperature may also affect exacerbations (Donaldson *et al.*, 1999) and viral infections are more common in the winter months (Wedzicha & Donaldson, 2003).

Siafakas *et al.* (1995) recognised that co-morbid conditions such as heart failure, pneumonia and pulmonary embolism can also provoke exacerbations. Research studies are ongoing but it is acknowledged that a cause cannot be identified in around one-third of cases (Sapey & Stockley, 2006).

Pathophysiology

Patho-physiology

The diverse pathophysiology of stable COPD is reflected in the varied manifestation of exacerbations. Essentially, in an exacerbation the expiratory airflow limitation increases (above the patient's usual) so it becomes much harder for patients to breathe out. The airway and systemic inflammation present in stable COPD is amplified during exacerbations (Sapey & Stockley, 2006). The increased airway inflammation produces airway wall oedema and thickening, bronchoconstriction and mucus production. This causes more airway resistance and so increases expiratory flow limitation. The time needed to empty the lungs becomes longer and so the amount of air left in the lungs after breathing out (end expired lung volume) also increases resulting in greater hyperinflation (above the patient's usual). The rise in hyperinflation means the patient has increased work of respiratory muscles and oxygen consumption (Tsoumakidou & Siafakas, 2006). Expiratory airflow limitation and hyperinflation lead to serious problems in severe exacerbations and it is likely that less severe exacerbations work in a similar way but to a lesser degree (O'Donnell & Parker, 2006).

Symptoms

Symptoms

An exacerbation cannot be typified by one symptom alone as they vary in severity and from one patient to another. Most commonly the symptoms are increased breathlessness, increased sputum volume and increased sputum purulence. Other symptoms can involve a cough which may be increased or a new feature, cold symptoms and sore throat, wheeze, ankle swelling, chest tightness, fatigue, a reduced ability to exercise or carry out usual activities, fluid retention and confusion (NICE, 2004). There may be additional non-specific symptoms such as general malaise, depression, sleepiness and insomnia (GOLD, 2005).

Assessment

Assessment

A full medical history, the history of the presenting complaint, details and duration of the current symptoms should be taken to assess the severity of the exacerbation. Careful questioning is often necessary to elicit the precise symptom changes from the patient's normal stable state, with special interest in breathlessness, sputum volume and purulence. The severity of the underlying COPD should be established as it will be closely related to the significance of the exacerbation; any reduction in function will have a greater impact on a patient with severe disease than on a patient with mild disease (Rodriguez-Roisin, 2000).

It is helpful to review any recent investigation results that are available, for example spirometry, arterial blood gases or pulse oximetry. The patient's current drug treatment can give some indication of the disease stage, although this cannot be relied on as they may not have been treated appropriately. Patients having home nebulised therapy are usually thought to have more severe disease but the nebuliser compressor may have been bought by the patient and started without accurate assessment. Oxygen therapy especially causes confusion. Short burst oxygen may have been prescribed for patients with moderate COPD. Having had

Managing an exacerbation in primary care

this for several years (a long time) can be understood to mean Long-term Oxygen Therapy (LTOT) which is actually quite different and indicates more severe disease.

Patient examination should include observation of respiratory, cardiovascular and general signs to assess the severity of the clinical features of COPD.

Respiratory signs are:
- tachypnoea (respiratory rate more than 30 bpm)
- shallow breathing
- use of accessory muscles (sternocleidomastoid and scalenes)
- wheezing
- paradoxical (asymmetrical) chest wall movements
- diminished or absent breath sounds
- hyper-resonance on percussion
- pursed lip breathing (adopted naturally by some patients who breathe out against pursed lips in an attempt to prevent air trapping).

Cardiovascular signs are:
- tachycardia (heart rate more than 100 bpm)
- arrhythmias
- abnormal blood pressure
- right heart failure, for instance raised jugular venous pressure (JVP), enlarged liver, ankle and sacral oedema.

Two important general signs are:
- central cyanosis (dusky blue skin on the lips and in the mouth) indicating hypoxia
- reduced alertness along with a bounding pulse, vasodilation (warm flushed peripheries) and flapping tremor (asterixis), suggesting carbon dioxide retention.

The presence of either of these signs indicates that immediate hospital assessment should be arranged (Hansel & Barnes, 2004).

Pulse oximetry enables non-invasive monitoring of the peripheral oxygen saturation. It is a useful aid when assessing hypoxia, especially when comparison to the patient's usual level is available, as many COPD patients will normally have low oxygen levels. Oxygen saturation of less than 92 per cent needs further investigation unless this is the patient's norm. Pulse oximetry has limitations as erroneous readings can be caused by poor perfusion, movement, anaemia, nail varnish and other factors. Be aware that pulse oximetry gives no information about the carbon dioxide level which may be rising insidiously. Only arterial blood gases provide this information exactly. For these reasons the use of pulse oximetry alone is only recommended for mild exacerbations (Rodriguez-Roisin, 2006).

As this patient group is generally older and frequently has several co-morbidities there are many differential diagnoses. The main ones are pneumonia, pneumothorax, pulmonary embolism, pleural effusion, pulmonary oedema/left ventricular failure, lung cancer, myocardial infarction, upper airway obstruction, recurrent aspiration, chest trauma, rib fractures, cardiac arrhythmias and adverse effects of sedatives. Considerable caution is required with this vulnerable group of patients as secondary problems could be developing alongside the exacerbation.

A most important decision is whether the patient can be treated at home or needs hospital admission. This will depend on many factors such as: the severity of the exacerbation and underlying COPD, any diagnostic uncertainty, the significance of any co-morbid conditions, the extent of support available from the patient's family or carers or from community nursing services and the patient's individual home circumstances. NICE (2004) makes clear recommendations regarding the factors which should be considered in making this decision. These include:

- Can the patient cope at home?
- What are their social circumstances?
- How severe is the breathlessness?
- What is the patient's general condition?
- Are there significant co-morbidities?
- Is the patient mobile or confined to bed?
- Is there any cyanosis present?
- Is there any worsening of peripheral oedema?
- Is the patient alert or confused?
- Did the symptoms come on rapidly?
- Is the patient already receiving LTOT?

The decision to admit patients to hospital may be due to social circumstances as much as for more intensive medical intervention. There are occasions when patients who are severely ill may refuse hospital admission preferring to stay at home. Often they have discussed this at length with their primary care physician or hospital consultant and are fully aware of the consequences. The wishes of these patients should be respected, if at all possible, and supported by community palliative care and nursing teams.

Hospital at Home and Early Discharge Services

HAH & EDS

Hospital at Home (HAH) and Early Discharge Services (EDS) have been extensively introduced throughout the UK and other countries, as an alternative way of managing patients who would usually need hospital admission or longer stay due to an exacerbation of COPD. There are many different models in use, some schemes assessing patients in hospital and then caring for them in the community; others discharging patients from hospital early with close monitoring at home. Typically, the HAH and EDS teams are multidisciplinary combinations comprising of respiratory specialist nurses, district nurses, doctors, physiotherapists, occupational therapists and social workers who together provide a comprehensive package of care. Ideally the teams will have good links with other key healthcare professionals such as community matrons and the specialist nurses for the common co-morbidities like heart failure and diabetes.

Given the rising costs and pressure on hospital beds there is a great deal of enthusiasm for developing an effective service which reduces inpatient bed days. Ram *et al.* (2004) conducted a systematic review of HAH services which assessed patients with exacerbations of COPD at hospital, then managed the patient at home with close follow-up. The review concluded that these services are a safe and effective method of caring for patients who would otherwise have been admitted to hospital. Not surprisingly, many patients prefer to avoid a hospital admission and be cared for in their own homes. Ojoo *et al.* (2002) showed that, after using a domiciliary service, both patients' and carers' perceptions of benefit were reinforced by their experiences. NICE (2004) recommends that patient preference regarding home or hospital treatment should be considered. A randomised controlled trial carried out by Skwarska *et al.* (2000) found that HAH provisions were cost effective but Ram *et al.* (2004) were unable to draw any conclusions about cost effectiveness. As these schemes develop additional research is essential to refine the patient selection criteria and team membership and to discover which models of care provide the most benefit for which groups of patients.

Investigations and treatment

The patient's respiratory rate, pulse and temperature should be recorded. Few other investigations are necessary for exacerbations in primary care. Pulse oximetry is useful when assessing a more severe exacerbation and will contribute to the decision as to where best to treat the patient. Sputum specimens for culture are not recommended routinely because empirical treatment is effective if it is prescribed promptly when sputum is purulent (NICE, 2004). Assessment of peak flow or spirometry is not usually valuable during exacerbations as changes are small and performing the test when unwell is difficult (Hurst & Wedzicha, 2004).

The aims of treatment are to relieve the symptoms, treat the cause if it is known, identify promptly any deterioration and recognise the need for further support or hospital admission.

Bronchodilators

Broncho-dilators

Inhaled short-acting beta$_2$-agonists (SABAs) such as salbutamol or terbutaline and anticholinergic agents such as ipratropium bromide are the primary treatment for exacerbations; they reduce symptoms and reduce airflow obstruction (Rodriguez-Roisin, 2006). Most patients will already be on inhaled bronchodilators. If not, these should be initiated and, if so, the dose and/or frequency of the usual therapy should be increased. It is essential to establish the correct starting point. Ask the patient to tell you how much of each inhaler they are currently taking. Do not assume that patients are taking their inhalers as prescribed. Intentionally or mistakenly, they frequently stray away from their prescribed doses.

No difference in bronchodilation during exacerbations has been established between SABAs and anticholinergic agents or any synergistic effect (McCrory & Brown, 2002). However Salpeter *et al.* (2004) noted that SABA may increase the risk of cardiovascular events. This would be especially important to patients with co-existing heart disease. The GOLD (2005) guidelines recommend adding an anticholinergic if not already in use whilst Rodriguez-Roisin (2006) proposes that this remains empirical.

Managing an exacerbation in primary care

Currently there is no evidence for the place of long-acting bronchodilators in exacerbations (Hurst & Wedzicha, 2004). Note that the anticholinergic agents, ipratropium bromide (short-acting) and tiotropium (long-acting) should not be used concurrently, unlike the beta-agonists salbutamol (short-acting) and salmeterol (long-acting) which can be used at the same time. The position of aminophylline in treating exacerbations is presently in dispute (Barr *et al.*, 2003) but it is not indicated for exacerbations managed in the community.

Increasing breathlessness may mean that the patient is unable to use their usual inhaler device effectively. It is crucial to reconsider the patient's inhaler device and technique during an exacerbation. A device which is normally satisfactory can be too difficult when patients are very breathless. Patients may overestimate their ability to take their inhalers correctly; the only way to be sure they can use the device is by watching their technique.

Nebulisers

In more severe exacerbations, nebulised therapy can be sometimes be useful if a compressor loan can be arranged. A nebuliser uses a gas (air or oxygen) to change a liquid drug into an aerosol to be inhaled. At home this is done by a portable air compressor, a nebuliser acorn, tubing and a mask or mouthpiece. It may be easier for patients to take their medication using a nebuliser but they can have problems with using the equipment, loading the drug, cleaning and drying the nebuliser acorn. Again help or supervision from a relative or carer is often required. A mask or mouthpiece can be used. The mask is easier to use when unwell but some patients find the mask claustrophobic and prefer a mouthpiece. A mouthpiece should be used with ipratropium bromide to prevent the nebulised drug getting into the eyes, which can lead to glaucoma.

Nebulisers for patients with COPD should only be driven by an air compressor. It is possible to run them from a portable oxygen cylinder but oxygen must not be used under these circumstances due to the risk of carbon dioxide retention (discussed below). Patients and carers should be warned only to use the air compressor. If the patient is already using a home nebuliser it is always worth inspecting this closely as often servicing and maintenance are neglected.

Management of COPD in primary and secondary care

Patients have been known to obtain air compressors and nebuliser solutions in extraordinary ways, such as from car boot sales or deceased relatives. Some incorrectly attempt to use nebulised therapy via oxygen concentrators or a tyre inflator. Airflow of between 6 and 8 l/min is needed to produce drug particles small enough to breathe in. Clear written information and training on the use and cleaning of nebulisers ought to be provided as poor hygiene can lead to further infection. The acorn should be washed and left to dry after each use. Oxygen can be continued during nebulisation via nasal cannula. If nebulised therapy is used the patient should be changed back to inhalers as soon as possible. Many GPs no longer keep nebulisers due to the practicalities of cleaning them between patients, the maintenance required and the lack of evidence of superiority over the MDI and spacer (Brocklebank *et al.*, 2001).

The usual inhaled doses for inhaled short-acting bronchodilators are beta$_2$-agonists salbutamol 200 micrograms four times a day and terbutaline sulphate 500 micrograms four times a day, and anticholinergic bronchodilator ipratropium bromide 40 micrograms four times a day. In practice these doses are often increased during exacerbations to salbutamol 400 micrograms four times a day or terbutaline sulphate 1 mg four times a day and ipratropium bromide 80 micrograms four times a day, but these doses are unlicensed and may cause increased side effects.

The usual nebulised doses for short-acting bronchodilators are salbutamol 2.5 to 5 mg four times a day, terbutaline sulphate 5 to 10 mg four times a day and ipratropium bromide 250 to 500 micrograms four times a day (British National Formulary 2006 – www.bnf.org, accessed 1.8.07).

Antibiotics

Antibiotics are used extensively in exacerbations of COPD but their use remains contentious. Many exacerbations have viral or non-infective causes so antibiotic treatment would not seem suitable and there are concerns regarding the growing resistance to common antibiotics. Ram *et al.* (2006) performed a systematic review which supports the use of antibiotics for patients with COPD exacerbations who have increased cough and sputum purulence and are moderately or severely ill. NICE (2004) advocate antibiotics to treat exacerbations associated with more

Antibiotics

purulent sputum but not those without, unless there is radiological evidence or clinical signs of pneumonia.

The choice of antibiotic depends upon the patterns of bacterial sensitivity and resistance in the area so should be in accordance with local microbiologist guidance. Generally broad-spectrum agents are adequate and amoxicillin is a suitable first choice. Patients should have a full therapeutic course, usually of seven days. If the infection is not resolving, re-evaluate the patient and, if indicated, send a sputum specimen for culture and sensitivity testing to ensure appropriate treatment. Newer second choice agents such as co-amoxiclav must only be used when there is lack of clinical response to first-choice agent or bacteriological evidence of resistance.

Oral corticosteroids

Oral cortico-steroids

The role of oral steroids for COPD exacerbations has been uncertain in primary care for many years. The benefit of systemic corticosteroids for hospital patients with moderate to severe exacerbations in reducing recovery time and restoring lung function has now been recognised, although adverse effects, most commonly hyperglycaemia, were increased (Wood-Baker *et al.*, 2005). Thompson *et al.* (1996) and Seemungal *et al.* (2000) demonstrated comparable effects for patients cared for in the community.

For milder exacerbations corticosteroid use is not as clear. The current shift towards caring for more patients in their own homes and the growth of HAH and EDS has led to more poorly patients in the community and a blurring of the distinction between hospital and community patients. NICE (2004) recommend that oral corticosteroids should be considered in community patients who have a significant increase in breathlessness interfering with their daily activities, provided there is no major contra-indication. GOLD guidelines (2005) suggest systemic corticosteroids if the patient's FEV_1 is less than 50 per cent. The optimum dose and duration has not yet been established. NICE (2004) advise 30 mg prednisolone for 7 to 14 days whereas GOLD (2005) suggests 40 mg prednisolone for ten days, which should not be continued after the exacerbation.

Longer oral corticosteroid courses have no benefit and may increase side effects and, provided the course has been less than three weeks, there is usually no need to taper off the dose (Currie

& Wedzicha, 2006). It is important to ensure that the patient knows why, how and when to stop oral corticosteroids. Those requiring repeated corticosteroid courses should be monitored for side effects and considered for osteoporosis prophylaxis (NICE, 2004). There is no place for starting inhaled corticosteroids in an exacerbation but patients already taking them should continue (Hurst & Wedzicha, 2004).

Oxygen

Oxygen

Patients with exacerbations of COPD who develop hypoxia and need oxygen therapy should only be given controlled rates of oxygen and be very closely observed due to the danger of carbon dioxide retention and acidosis. In a healthy person the stimulus to breathe comes from the rising level of carbon dioxide in the body. In a person with COPD the carbon dioxide levels may become permanently high; their body becomes accustomed to this so the stimulus to breathe changes and comes from low oxygen levels. This is known as 'hypoxic drive'. Giving too much oxygen to this patient is therefore dangerous. Hypoxia is a major risk but too much oxygen is unsafe for some patients with respiratory failure. Patients who have oxygen at home must be warned that increasing the flow rate may make their condition worse. A patient with an exacerbation of COPD may need arterial blood gas monitoring and careful supervision. If so, this requires hospital admission. Administration of oxygen therapy before or during transfer to hospital must be done with caution as uncontrolled oxygen can suppress the respiratory drive, cause carbon dioxide narcosis and even respiratory arrest (NICE, 2004). Murphy *et al.* (2001) advise that oxygen saturations should be maintained between 90 and 92 per cent during ambulance journeys pre-hospital assessment.

Additional therapies

Additional therapies

Any co-existing conditions may have contributed to, or be affected by, the COPD exacerbation. These will need attention as adjustments to the current treatment may be necessary. Other supportive care may include optimising and monitoring fluid balance and giving nutritional supplements. If the heart function is impaired, shown by a raised JVP and peripheral oedema, diuretics may be indicated. Beware that ankle oedema has not just developed because the patient has been too breathless to move as much as usual (see Chapter 7). Think about anticoagulant prophylaxis against venous thrombosis especially if the patient is known to have polycythaemia or is immobile. Patients should avoid taking sedatives or hypnotics. Cough suppressants are contraindicated as cough and expectoration are a necessary part of clearing secretions (Hurst and Wedzicha, 2004).

Care at home

Care at home

Attention has to be given to the patient's home circumstances. The exacerbation will reduce their ability to move about, attend to personal hygiene and prepare meals or drinks. The patient may have been struggling to manage alone and had difficulties with shopping and personal care for some time. Extra help will probably be needed and often this is at hand from the patient's own family or friends. If not, support must be arranged.

Even when relatives are living with a patient or nearby, they may not be able or suitable to provide help. Input from social services should be arranged to provide the requisite care. This is fundamental as good nutrition and hydration are essential to aid recovery. Many patients with COPD are elderly with co-morbidities making them a vulnerable group. Be alert as some will have underlying problems such as constipation or urinary tract infection which will be a contributing difficulty but can usually be easily alleviated.

Review

The timing of patient review depends upon the clinical appraisal of the exacerbation and the patient's circumstances. Mild exacerbations may not need review until the patient has recovered and can be followed up by the primary care physician. Other cases will require a review within hours to ensure that bronchodilators have relieved symptoms and that treatment has begun to take effect. Patients near the threshold for hospital admission at original assessment and those with no or less capable support at home should be most closely monitored. It is always best to review sooner if there are any doubts.

Failure to respond to treatment, an increase in symptoms or the onset of new signs such as cyanosis or peripheral oedema will necessitate hospital assessment. If the patient has decided not to have a hospital admission or invasive treatment, palliative care support should be arranged. Due to diverse initiatives in different areas of the country the community support available varies. It is valuable to know the local services and arrangements. Comprehensive instructions must be left so that patients and carers know when they should expect to feel better and how to get help if they do not improve or if they become worse. Ensure that essential contact details are clearly written down.

Follow-up

Follow-up

Appropriate follow-up should be arranged, usually at the surgery, to ensure that the exacerbation has fully resolved. The patient should be established on optimal therapy and so will require a full review. This may include smoking cessation advice and support, spirometry, pulse oximetry, Medical Research Council (MRC) dyspnoea scale scoring, symptom control, changes to medication and a check on inhaler technique. Also it is essential to address the patient's nutritional status and whether they are depressed. They could be suitable for pulmonary rehabilitation, or benefit from a multi-disciplinary or secondary care referral, perhaps for long-term oxygen assessment? Any required input from social services and occupational therapy assessment should also be addressed. The patient ought to be included on the practice COPD register which will make sure they are called for annual or twice-yearly review and influenza and pneumococcal vaccination.

Prevention

Prevention

Not all patients with COPD have frequent exacerbations but, not surprisingly, those who do have a worse health status and quality of life (Spencer *et al.*, 2004). Preventing or reducing the impact of exacerbations is a key aim of health professionals caring for people with COPD and substantial research is ongoing to this end. The main areas of investigation are influenza and pneumococcal vaccinations, pharmacological interventions and pulmonary rehabilitation.

Influenza vaccination has been shown to reduce exacerbations (Poole *et al.*, 2006) but pneumococcal vaccination has shown only small benefits and randomised controlled trials are needed (Granger *et al.*, 2006). Both vaccines are recommended for COPD patients by the NICE guidelines (2004).

Long-acting bronchodilators and inhaled corticosteroids have demonstrated reductions in exacerbations (Sin, *et al.*, 2003) and should be considered for all patients with moderate to severe COPD. Phosphodiesterase inhibitors, mucolytics and antioxidants require further study (Scott *et al.*, 2006).

Pulmonary rehabilitation is an exercise and education programme, well established as successful in improving the lives of people with COPD. Its effectiveness in reducing patients exacerbations is not well studied but Foglio *et al.* (1999) found that exacerbations were less frequent in patients who had attended pulmonary rehabilitation and Griffiths *et al.* (2000) found that rehabilitation resulted in shorter hospital stays. The importance of exercise was confirmed in a study by Garcia-Aymerich *et al.* (2006) who found that people with COPD who undertake regular physical activity have a lower risk of COPD-related hospital admission and death.

Optimising the patient's stable COPD management would be good practice and also providing advice on maintaining a healthy lifestyle, especially smoking cessation, healthy eating and exercise.

Self-management

Self-management

Self-management aims to prevent exacerbations by lifestyle adjustments and enable patients with skills to treat them promptly. Early treatment of a COPD exacerbation leads to a quicker recovery and patients who have better treated exacerbations have a better quality of life (Wilkinson *et al.*, 2004).

Many patients are able to recognise their own particular signs and symptoms of a developing exacerbation. Once known, this can lead them to start earlier treatment. It is known that patients who exacerbate frequently are likely to continue to do so

Management of COPD in primary and secondary care

(Wedzicha & Donaldson, 2003). Patients often become experts in managing their own disease so it is logical to build on this by providing education and encouraging self-management. This has been shown to work effectively in asthma but a COPD exacerbation is not so easily identified or easily treated as asthma.

Talking with patients after their exacerbation can allow them to identify key factors in its progression. Some patients recognise the exacerbation but believe it is inescapable and that nothing can be done to alleviate the symptoms. As a result they don't contact a health professional until they are very unwell and then may have to be admitted to hospital. Identifying the significant symptoms and developing a clear plan of action together could enable the patient to forestall future exacerbations. The evidence evaluating structured education and self-management programmes has produced diverse results. Some studies of self-management programmes found they resulted in more appropriate interventions, reduced healthcare use, better health status and less all-cause hospitalisation (Wood-Baker *et al.*, 2006; Bourbeau *et al.*, 2003; Gadoury *et al.*, 2005). However Monninkhof *et al.* (2003) found no positive effects and Martin *et al.* (2004) saw no improvement in healthcare use or quality of life. A systematic review by Taylor *et al.* (2005) concluded that the data was too sparse to exclude benefit or harm from the interventions.

The NICE guidelines (2004) advocate that COPD patients should be given a self-management plan that allows them to respond quickly to the symptoms of an exacerbation. A self-management plan should teach patients when and how to:

- adjust their bronchodilators to control increased breathlessness
- start oral corticosteroids if they are unable to carry out activities of daily life (unless contraindicated)
- start antibiotics if their sputum is purulent.

Courses of antibiotics and oral steroids should be kept at home ready for use when indicated and the appropriate use of these must be monitored. Patients are advised when to seek help from health professionals if their symptoms do not improve. Individual management plans, effective patient education and the development of tools for teaching are suggested by GOLD (2005) as avenues warranting future research.

References

Barr, R.G., Rowe, B.H. and Camargo, C.A. (2003). Methylxanthines for exacerbations of Chronic Obstructive Pulmonary Disease: Meta-analysis of randomised trials. *British Medical Journal*, 327, 643–653.

Bourbeau, J., Julien, M., Maltais, F., Rouleau, M., Beaupre, A., Begin, R., Renzi, P., Nault, D., Borycki, E., Schwartzman, K., Sing, R. and Collet, J.P. for the Chronic Obstructive Pulmonary Disease Axis of the Respiratory Network Fonds de la Recherche en Santé du Quebec (FRSQ) (2003). Reduction of hospital utilization in patients with Chronic Obstructive Pulmonary Disease: A disease specific self-management intervention. *Archives of International Medicine*, 163(5), 585–591.

Brocklebank, D., Ram, F., Wright, J., Barry, P., Cates, C., Davies, L., Douglas, G., Murers, M., Smith, D. and White, J. (2001). Comparison of the effectiveness of inhaler devices in asthma and Chronic Obstructive Pulmonary Disease: A systematic review of the literature. *Health Technology Assessment*, 5(26), 1–149.

Currie, G.P. and Wedzicha, J.A. (2006). Acute exacerbations. *British Medical Journal*, 333, 87

Donaldson, G.C., Seemungal, T.A.R., Jeffries, D.J. and Wedzicha, J.A. (1999). Effect of temperature on lung function and symptoms in chronic obstructive pulmonary disease. *European Respiratory Journal*, 13(4), 844–849.

Donaldson, G.C., Seemungal, T.A.R., Bhowmik, A. and Wedzicha, J.A. (2002). Relationship between exacerbation frequency and lung function decline in chronic obstructive pulmonary disease. *Thorax*, 57(10), 847–852.

Donaldson, G.C. and Wedzicha, J.A. (2006). COPD exacerbations. 1: Epidemiology. *Thorax*, 61, 164–168.

Foglio, K., Bianchi, L., Bruletti, G., Battista, L., Pagani, M. and Amorosino, N. (1999). Long-term effectiveness of pulmonary rehabilitation in patients with chronic airways disease. *European Respiratory Journal*, 13, 125–132.

Gadoury, M.A., Schwartzman, K., Rouleau, M., Maltais, F., Julien, M., Beaupre, A., Renzi, P., Begin, R., Nault, D., Bourbeau, J. for the Chronic Obstructive Pulmonary Disease Axis of the Respiratory Network Fonds de la Recherche en Santé du Quebec (FRSQ) (2005). Self-management reduces both short and long-term hospitalisation in COPD. *European Respiratory Journal*, 26(5), 853–857.

Garcia-Aymerich, J., Lange, P., Benet, M., Schnohr, P. and Anto, J.M. (2006) Regular physical activity reduces hospital admission and mortality in Chronic Obstructive Pulmonary Disease: A population based cohort study. *Thorax*, 61, 772–778.

Global Initiative for Chronic Obstructive Lung Disease (GOLD) (2006) *Global Strategy for the Diagnosis, Management and Prevention of Chronic Obstructive Pulmonary Disease*. Workshop Report November 2006. Bethesda: NLHBI/WHO.

Granger, R., Walters, J., Poole, P.J., Lasserson, T.J., Mangtani, P., Cates, J. and Wood-Baker, R. (2006). Injectable vaccines for preventing pneumococcal infection in patients with chronic obstructive pulmonary disease (Cochrane Review). *The Cochrane Library*, 4.

Greenberg, S B., Allen, M., Wilson, J. and Atmar, R. L. (2000). Respiratory viral infections in adults with and without chronic obstructive pulmonary disease. *American Journal of Respiratory and Critical Care Medicine*, 162, 167–173.

Griffiths, T.L., Burr, M.L., Campbell, I.A., Lewis-Jenkins, V., Mullins, J., Shields, K., Turner-Lawor, P., Payne, N., Newcombe, R. and Lonescu, A. (2000) Results at one year of outpatient multidisciplinary pulmonary rehabilitation. *The Lancet*, 355, 362–368.

Hansel, T.T. and Barnes, P.J. (2004). *An Atlas of Chronic Obstructive Pulmonary Disease*. London: Parthenon Publishing Group.

Hurst, J.R. and Wedzicha, J.A. (2004) Chronic Obstructive Pulmonary Disease: The clinical management of an acute exacerbation. *Postgraduate Medicine Journal*, 80, 497–505

MacNee, W. (2003). Acute exacerbations of COPD. *Swiss Medicine Weekly*, 133, 247–257.

Martin, I.R., McNamara, D., Sutherland, F.R., Tilyard, M.W. and Taylor, D.R. (2004). Care plans for acutely deteriorating COPD: A randomised controlled trial. *Chronic Respiratory Disease*, 1(4), 191–195.

McCrory, D.C. and Brown, C.D. (2002). Anti-cholinergic bronchodilators versus beta$_2$-sympathomimetic agents for acute exacerbations of chronic obstructive pulmonary disease (Cochrane Review). *The Cochrane Library*, 4.

Monninkhof, E., van der Valk, P., van der Palen, J., van Herwaarden, C. and Zielhuis, G. (2003) Effects of a comprehensive self-management programme in patients with chronic obstructive pulmonary disease. *European Respiratory Journal*, 22(5), 815–820.

Murphy, R., Mackway-Jones, K., Sammy, I., Driscoll, P., Gray, A., O'Driscoll, R., O'Reilly, J., Niven, R., Bentley, A., Brear, G. and Kishen, R. (2001). Emergency oxygen therapy for the breathless patient. Guidelines prepared by the North West Oxygen Group. *Emergency Medicine Journal*, 18, 421–423.

National Institute for Health and Clinical Excellence (NICE) (2004). Chronic Obstructive Pulmonary Disease: National clinical guideline for management of chronic obstructive pulmonary disease in adults in primary and secondary care. *Thorax*, 59 (Suppl. 1), 1–232.

O'Donnell, D.E. and Parker, C.M. (2006). COPD exacerbations. 3: Pathophysiology. *Thorax*, 61, 354–361.

Ojoo, J.C., Moon, T., Mcglone, S., Martin, K., Gardiner, E.D., Greenstone, M.A. and Morice, A.H. (2002). Patients' and carers' preferences on two models of care for acute exacerbations of COPD: Results of a randomised control trial. *Thorax*, 57, 167–169.

Patel, I.S., Seemungal, T.A.R., Wilks, M., Lloyd-Owen, S.J., Donaldson, G.C. and Wedzicha, J.A. (2002). Relationship between bacterial colonisation and the frequency, characteristics and severity of COPD exacerbation. *Thorax*, 57, 759–764.

Poole, P.J., Chacko, E., Wood-Baker, R.W. and Cates, C.J. (2006). Influenza vaccine for patients with chronic obstructive pulmonary disease (Cochrane Review). *The Cochrane Library*, 1.

Ram, F.S., Rodriguez-Roisin, R., Granados-Navarrete, A., Garcia-Aymerich, J. and Barnes, P. (2006). Antibiotics for exacerbations of chronic obstructive pulmonary disease (Cochrane Review). *The Cochrane Library*, 2.

Ram, F., Wedzicha, J., Wright, J. and Greenstone, M. (2004). Hospital at home for patients with acute exacerbations of COPD: Systematic review of evidence. *British Medical Journal*, 329, 315–319.

Rodriguez-Roisin, R. (2000) Towards a consensus definition for COPD exacerbations. *Chest*, 117, S398S–S401.

Rodriguez-Roisin, R. (2006) COPD exacerbations. 5: Management. *Thorax*, 61, 535–544.

Salpeter, S.R., Ormiston, T.M. and Salpeter, E.E. (2004). Cardiovascular effects of beta-agonists in patients with asthma and COPD: A meta-analysis. *Chest*, 125(6), 2309–2321.

Sapey, E. and Stockley, R.A. (2006). COPD exacerbations. 2: Aetiology. *Thorax*, 61, 250–258.

Scott, S., Walker, P. and Calverley, P.M.A. (2006). COPD exacerbations. 4: Prevention. *Thorax*, 61, 440–447.

Seemungal, T.A.R., Donaldson, C.G., Bhowmik, A., Jeffries, D.J. and Wedzicha, J.A. (2000). Time course and recovery of exacerbations in patients with chronic obstructive pulmonary disease. *American Journal of Respiratory and Critical Care Medicine*, 161(5), 1608–1613.

Seemungal, T.A.R., Donaldson, C.G., Paul, E.A., Bestall, J.C., Jeffries, D.J. and Wedzicha J.A. (1998). Effect of exacerbation on quality of life in patients with chronic obstructive pulmonary disease. *American Journal of Respiratory and Critical Care Medicine*, 157, 1418–1422.

Siafakas, N.M., Vermeire, P., Pride, N.B., Paoletti, P., Gibson, J., Howard, P., Yernault, J.C., Decramer, M., Higenbottam, T., Postma, D.S. and Rees, J. on behalf of the European Respiratory Society Task Force. (1995). Optimal assessment and management of chronic obstructive pulmonary disease (COPD). *European Respiratory Journal*, 8, 1398–1420.

Sin, D.D., McAlister, F.A., Man, S.F., Anthonisen, N.R. (2003). Contemporary management of Chronic Obstructive Pulmonary Disease: Scientific review. *Journal of the American Medical Association*, 290(17), 2301–2312.

Skwarska, E., Cohen, G., Skwarski, K.M., Lamb, C., Bushell, D., Parker, S. and Macnee, W. (2000). Randomised controlled trial of supported discharge in patients with exacerbations of chronic obstructive pulmonary disease. *Thorax*, 55, 907–912.

Spencer, S., Calverley, P.M.A., Burge, P.S.and Jones, P.W. (2004). Impact of preventing exacerbations on deterioration of health status in COPD. *European Respiratory Journal*, 23, 698–702.

Taylor, S., Candy, B., Bryar, R.M., Ramsay, J., Vrijhoef, H.J.M., Esmond, G., Wedzicha, J.A. and Griffiths, C.J. (2005). Effectiveness of innovations in nurse-led chronic disease management for patients with Chronic Obstructive Pulmonary Disease: Systematic review of evidence. *British Medical Journal*, 331, 485–494.

Thompson, W.H., Nielson, C.P., Carvalho, P., Charan, N.B. and Crowley, J.J. (1996). Controlled trial of oral prednisolone in outpatients with acute COPD exacerbations. *American Journal of Respiratory and Critical Care Medicine*, 154, 407–412.

Tsoumakidou, M. and Siafakas, N.M. (2006). Novel insights into the aetiology and pathophysiology of increased airway inflammation during COPD exacerbations. *Respiratory Research*, 7, 80–86.

Wedzicha, J.A. (2002). Exacerbations: etiology and pathophysiologic mechanisms. *Chest*, 121(5), S136S–S141.

Wedzicha, J.A. (2004). Role of viruses in exacerbations of chronic obstructive pulmonary disease. *Proceedings of the American Thoracic Society*, 1, 115–120.

Wedzicha, J.A. and Donaldson, G.C.(2003). Exacerbations of chronic obstructive pulmonary disease. *Respiratory Care*, 48(12), 1204–1215.

Wilkinson, T.M.A., Donaldson, G.C., Hurst, J.R., Seemungal, T.A.R. and Wedzicha, J.A. (2004). Early therapy improves outcomes of exacerbations of chronic obstructive pulmonary disease. *American Journal of Respiratory and Critical Care Medicine*, 169, 1298–1303.

Wood-Baker, R.R., Gibson, P.G., Hannay, M., Walters, E.H. and Walters, J.A. (2005). Systemic corticosteroids for acute exacerbations of chronic obstructive pulmonary disease (Cochrane Review). *The Cochrane Library*, 1.

Wood-Baker, R.R., Mcglone, S., Venn, A., Walters, E.H. (2006). Written action plans in chronic obstructive pulmonary disease increase appropriate treatment for acute exacerbations. *Respirology*, 11(5), 619–626.

Zalacain, R., Sobradillo, V., Amilibia, J., Baron, J., Achotegui, V., Pijoan, J.I. and Llorente, J.L. (1999). Predisposing factors to bacterial colonisation in chronic obstructive pulmonary disease. *European Respiratory Journal*, 13, 343–348.

Chapter 7
Management of respiratory failure caused by exacerbations
Sue Meehan

Exacerbations of COPD requiring hospitalisation are serious and distressing events for both patients and carers, and they are clearly linked to increased morbidity and mortality. They can be defined as a sustained worsening of the patient's symptoms from the patient's usual stable state that is acute in onset (NICE, 2004). Common symptoms are worsening breathlessness, coughing and increased sputum production and change in sputum colour. Exacerbations can often be managed in the patient's home but they can lead to significant respiratory failure and may need to be managed in a hospital.

This chapter provides an introduction to the management of respiratory failure in hospital, including introductions to investigations such as blood gas analysis and interventions such as oxygen therapy, non-invasive ventilation (NIV) and, in particular, Bi-level Positive Airway Pressure (BiPAP).

Before defining respiratory failure, it is important to have a basic understanding of two concepts: 'work of breathing' and 'V/Q ratio'.

Work of breathing

Work of breathing

Work of breathing clearly contributes to the development of respiratory failure during exacerbations of COPD. It is the amount of force needed to move a given volume of air into the lung with a relaxed chest wall. Obstructive airway diseases may raise respiratory work requirements excessively due to the presence of 'intrinsic PEEP' (positive end expiratory pressure) and hyperinflation and this is the most common cause of respiratory muscle fatigue. Hyperinflation and trapped air cause lowering of the diaphragm and expansion of the rib cage. This makes respiratory muscles inefficient as they cannot use their full range of movement and the patient tires more easily.

When patients have increased work of breathing they may develop a rapid respiratory rate (tachypnoea). Importantly, this will mean that the patient will have a reduced rest period between respirations, which will add to their fatigue. The patient will have to use accessory muscles and work much harder in order to breathe. This means that they will use more oxygen which will add to their respiratory failure.

V/Q ratio

V/Q ratio

V/Q means ventilation and perfusion. 'Ventilation' refers to the ventilation of alveoli during breathing and 'perfusion' refers to the perfusion of the pulmonary capillaries that surround the alveoli with blood. Clearly it is important that ventilation and perfusion occur at the same place, as this will enable gaseous exchange to take place. If an alveolus is ventilated with air but its blood capillaries are not perfused with blood, gaseous exchange cannot take place. Similarly if an alveolus is not ventilated with air, but its blood capillaries are perfused with blood, exchange will not occur. V/Q mismatching is therefore important.

V/Q matching is achieved by vasodilation or vasoconstriction of the capillaries that pass blood over alveoli. The smooth muscle in the walls of the arterioles and smaller airways contracts or relaxes in response to changes in the partial pressure of oxygen in alveoli.

A low V/Q ratio means that the alveoli are poorly ventilated, although pulmonary circulation is adequate. COPD is not the only cause of a low V/Q ratio. For example, the ratio can be reduced due to depression of the respiratory central drive, damage to the chest wall or paralysis of the ventilatory muscles. This is characterised by a lower alveolar PaO_2 and a higher than normal $PaCO_2$.

A high V/Q ratio indicates that the gas exchange is insufficient leading to hypoxia. Ventilation is adequate but the blood capillaries surrounding the alveoli are poorly perfused, perhaps due to shock, pulmonary emboli or haemorrhage.

Peripheral airways obstruction, parenchymal destruction and pulmonary vascular abnormalities in advanced COPD can alter V/Q matching and will reduce the lungs' capacity for gas exchange. In the more severe stages of the disorder a state of hypoxaemia develops at rest, and, eventually, the patient develops hypercapnia. Hypoxaemia is only present during exercise in the early stages of the disease, although a V/Q mismatch can occur at any stage (GOLD, 2006).

Body position may affect gas exchange by altering V/Q in the lung and this is clinically significant when managing patients. Those with unilateral lung disease benefit from being in a position with the healthy lung down (often referred to by physiotherapists as 'high side lying'), although regular position change is essential as secretions may gradually migrate to the lower lung. However, the patient in respiratory failure may benefit from being in the semi-erect or sitting position, supported with pillows, to facilitate and optimise V/Q matching.

What is respiratory failure?

Respiratory failure

Respiratory failure is defined as failure to maintain adequate gas exchange and is characterised by abnormalities of arterial blood gas tensions (BTS, 2002). To simplify this further it can be defined as the inability to maintain either the normal delivery of oxygen to the tissues or the normal removal of carbon dioxide (CO_2) from the tissues (Scanlan *et al.*, 1999). There are two classifications of respiratory failure: type I refers to the lungs failing to oxygenate arterial blood adequately, characterised by a PaO_2 of less than eight kiloPascals (kPa) with a normal or low $PaCO_2$, indicating a hypoxic state; type II relates to CO_2 retention, characterised by a PaO_2 of less than 8 kPa and a $PaCO_2$ of more than 6 kPa, indicating a hypercapnic state. In other words, a patient with type I respiratory failure will have too little oxygen in the blood, and is 'hypoxic', and a patient with type II respiratory failure will have too much CO_2 in their blood, and is 'hypercapnic'.

Respiratory failure can also be viewed as either an acute or chronic process. For example, patients with COPD may be constantly hypercapnic, which is chronic type II respiratory failure. This can develop into acute failure when there is a significant deterioration of their condition, for example during an exacerbation. Practitioners should be able to distinguish between these two states as the management is different.

Type I respiratory failure usually occurs when intrinsic lung disease has interfered with oxygen transfer in the lung only.

Conditions predisposing this include COPD, asthma, pulmonary embolism, pneumonia, pulmonary fibrosis, pneumothorax and adult respiratory distress syndrome (ARDS). Gas exchange is insufficient due to a V/Q mismatch and this, along with deterioration of the pre-disposing condition, can lead to hypoxia.

Typically COPD patients with type I respiratory failure are referred to as 'pink puffers' which sometimes describes their symptoms and appearance. 'Pink puffers' may be breathless and hyperventilating, using accessory muscles, yet they may have pink colouring. They may also have a hyperinflated chest and be underweight. Pursed lip breathing is not uncommon. It is important to note that not all type I respiratory failure patients will present like a 'pink puffer'.

Type II failure is usually caused by alveolar hypoventilation due to an exacerbation of COPD, neuromuscular disorders, opiate overdose, severe asthma, severe pneumonia and sleep disorders. The COPD patient with type II respiratory failure is not able to ventilate alveoli sufficiently to remove CO_2 due to exhaustion or obstructed airways, therefore a hypercapnic state develops (Lynes & Riches, 2003).

Type II respiratory failure can be acute, or it can be chronic. Indeed chronic respiratory failure can develop into acute respiratory failure during an exacerbation and this is sometimes called 'acute on chronic' respiratory failure. Chronic hypercapnic respiratory failure due to COPD has most probably developed over weeks or months; therefore the body has developed compensatory mechanisms to adapt to the disease. These compensatory mechanisms include a renal response in which the kidneys produce bicarbonate which enters the blood. This helps to elevate the blood pH, and can restore it to within normal limits. (See 'Blood gas analysis' below.)

A typical type II chronic respiratory failure patient is said to be less breathless than a type I patient; the chest is not hyperinflated but there is often peripheral oedema present along with cyanosis. The patient may be overweight. The accessory muscles may not be used. COPD patients with chronic type II respiratory failure have been unflatteringly but commonly referred to as 'blue bloaters' which sometimes describes their symptoms and appearance.

Table 7.1

Summary of type I and type II respiratory failure

	Type I *Acute (hypoxaemia) respiratory failure*	**Type II** *Hypercapnic respiratory failure*
CAUSES	Ventilation/perfusion (V/Q) mismatching	Decrease in central respiratory drive
	Increase in intrapulmonary shunt	Neuromuscular dysfunction
		Increased ventilatory load leading to exhaustion
		Increased alveolar dead space
RESULTS	Arterial $PaCO_2$ – normal or decreased	Arterial $PaCO_2$ (increased) > 6 kPa
	Arterial PaO_2 < 8 kPa	Arterial PaO_2 (decreased) < 8 kPa

To correctly diagnose, a full detailed history should be taken including physical examination, signs and symptoms experienced by the patient and arterial blood gas (ABG) analysis. The main clinical features of respiratory failure include headache, restlessness or agitation, confusion and decreased levels of consciousness. The patient may have an increased heart rate, chest pain/dysrhythmias, increased respiratory rate/depth/effort, use of accessory muscles of the neck shoulders and abdomen and decreased urinary output. They may have cool, clammy and pale skin and may be oedematous.

It is not possible to diagnose respiratory failure from symptoms and presentation alone; this should be considered in context with the patient history and confirmed by arterial blood gas analysis.

Blood gas analysis

Blood gas analysis

Arterial blood gases are the most sensitive indicator of respiratory function, particularly the levels of oxygen and CO_2, and can be used to initiate effective treatment. In order to interpret blood gases it is important to understand about acid-base balance and the role the lungs and kidneys play in maintaining it (Lynes, 2003).

Acids and bases

The pH is a measure of a solution's acidity or alkalinity and can have a value from 0 to 14. Pure water has a pH of seven which is neutral. A solution below seven is acidic – the lower the pH value, the more acidic. Likewise, a pH of over seven is alkali – the higher the pH value, the more alkaline.

To remain healthy, a person must be able to maintain homeostasis and have the ability to maintain a normal pH. If pH deviates from the normal limits essential body processes can be compromised leading to a life-threatening situation (Woodrow, 2004). An arterial blood pH of below 6.8 or above 7.8 is not compatible with life.

An acid is a chemical that can release hydrogen ions (H+). Strong acids release all of their H+ into a solution but weak acids do not release all. The more H+ in a solution the more acidic it becomes. Carbonic acid is an example of a weak acid that occurs naturally in the body.

A base or alkali can receive or absorb H+. Bicarbonate (HCO_3) is an example of a base and the more present in a solution the more alkaline it becomes.

When CO_2 is carried in the blood some of it combines with water to produce carbonic acid. Carbon dioxide + water = carbonic acid. Expressed as an equation this is:

$$CO_2 + H_2O = H_2CO_3.$$

The carbonic acid then dissociates (releases its hydrogen ion into the blood) which causes blood pH to drop. It follows that the more CO_2 in the blood, the more acid the blood is. If a patient has respiratory problems and retains CO_2 they can develop respiratory acidosis. The pH of blood is normally between 7.35 and 7.45. If a patient has too much CO_2 in the blood and the pH is below 7.35 they have developed respiratory acidosis.

It also follows that the less CO_2 in the blood the less acid the blood is. So, if a patient hyperventilates and there is too little CO_2 and therefore too little carbonic acid in the blood, the patient will have developed respiratory alkalosis (pH above 7.45).

If a patient has too much CO_2 in the blood and therefore too much acid, the body will respond by increasing the respiratory rate and will exhale the CO_2. However, if the patient has a respiratory or other problem, such as a head injury, they may not be able to do this. If this persists over hours or days the kidneys can produce bicarbonate (HCO_3.). The bicarbonate stabilises the carbonic acid in the blood, in other words it stops the carbonic acid dissociating and releasing its hydrogen ion. This means that, although the patient has too much CO_2 in the blood and therefore too much carbonic acid, the kidneys have produced bicarbonate which will ensure that the pH will be within normal limits (7.35 to 7.45) but will not be as high as 7.4. This situation is called 'compensated' respiratory acidosis, because the kidneys have compensated by producing bicarbonate. It takes a number of days for the kidneys to compensate in this way.

Acute type II (or hypercapnic) respiratory failure is characterised by arterial blood gas analysis showing a high $PaCO_2$, a low pH and normal bicarbonate – 'acute respiratory acidosis'. By contrast, chronic type II hypercapnic respiratory failure, is characterised by arterial blood gas analysis showing a high $PaCO_2$, pH within normal limits and high bicarbonate. The pH of blood will have returned to normal limits due to this 'renal compensation'. Therefore a high bicarbonate level will be evident on blood gas analysis. This is sometimes called 'compensated respiratory acidosis'. Patients with compensated respiratory acidosis are usually clinically stable but will have significant lung disease. Their arterial blood gases will always be deranged.

Sometimes patients with chronic type II respiratory failure can deteriorate, perhaps due to an exacerbation. When this happens it is called 'acute on chronic respiratory failure'. This indicates an acute deterioration of a pre-existing chronic hypercapnic respiratory failure. Arterial blood gases show a high $PaCO_2$, low pH and high bicarbonate. In this situation the pH is low despite the high bicarbonate levels. This may be due to an exacerbation of COPD, but it may also be due to injudicious use of oxygen therapy.

Acidosis and alkalosis can also be caused by non-respiratory problems, such as diabetic acidosis (ketoacidosis). In situations such as this, alterations in pH are not explained by levels of CO_2. For example, in diabetic acidosis the pH will be low but this is not explained by a high CO_2.

Interpretation of blood gases

Investigations only make sense in the context of clinical examination and blood gases may be misleading if relied upon in isolation. It is important to label the sample and complete any forms correctly. Details regarding the patient's condition should be recorded, especially if they are receiving oxygen therapy. The percentage of oxygen being given needs to be stated as this will have an effect on the results and subsequent treatment.

Normal values of blood gases vary from hospital to hospital, so it is important to familiarise yourself with the values used in your unit. The table below gives the values used in this chapter.

Table 7.2

Normal values of blood gases

	kPa (kiloPascals)	mm Hg
pH	7.35–7.45	
$PaCO_2$	4.7–6.0	35–45
PaO_2	11.3–14.0	80–100
HCO_3.	22–28 mEq/L	22–28 mEq/L
Base excess	+/- 2.5 mEq/L	+/- 2.5 mEq/L

In order to analyse and interpret blood gas results it is preferable to have a systematic process which involves five steps.

1. Look at the PaO_2 (oxygen). This indicates whether the patient is being oxygenated adequately. If it is below 8.0 kPa, then the patient is in respiratory failure, and if it is below 6.7 kPa, the patient is dangerously hypoxic

2. Look at the pH. Is it acid or alkali?

3. Look at the $PaCO_2$ (CO_2). Could this explain a low or raised pH? CO_2 combines with H_2O to form carbonic acid, so a high CO_2 would explain a low pH and a low CO_2 would explain a high pH. If the $PaCO_2$ explains why the pH is high or low, then the problem is likely to be respiratory in origin. If it does not then the problem is likely to be 'metabolic' or non-respiratory.

4. Look at the HCO_3. (bicarbonate). Could this explain a change in pH? A high bicarbonate may explain a high pH and a low bicarbonate may explain a low pH. If changes in bicarbonate levels explain pH the problem is likely to be metabolic or non-respiratory.

5. Assess for compensation. For example, the kidneys can compensate for respiratory acidosis by producing bicarbonate, which would mean that pH may be within normal limits despite a high $PaCO_2$. Similarly, the lungs can compensate for metabolic acidosis by 'blowing off' CO_2 resulting in a low $PaCO_2$.

Respiratory failure caused by exacerbations

For the purposes of this chapter we will ignore base excess. Base excess is a calculated figure that reflects the amount of acid or base that is needed to change one litre of blood to pH 7.4. This calculation is not relevant in assessing the impact of respiratory problems as it applies to metabolic imbalances (Scanlan *et al.*, 1999).

A COPD patient with compensated respiratory acidosis might have blood gas results similar to the example below.

pH	7.37
$PaCO_2$	8.29 kPa
PaO_2	7.9 kPa
$HCO_3.$	34 mEq/L

Use the steps to analyse the sample:

1. Look at the PaO_2. It is low but is there adequate oxygenation for a person with COPD?

2. Look at the pH. It is in the lower range of normal.

3. Look at the $PaCO_2$. It is high, indicating a respiratory acidosis.

4. Look at the $HCO_3.$. It is high, so the acidosis is not due to metabolic problems.

5. Assess for compensation. Because the $HCO_3.$ is high and the pH is within normal range, therefore a compensated respiratory acidosis is indicated.

Taking a sample

This procedure should be performed by a competent practitioner. The issue of competency is not discussed in this chapter but it is important that local policies and guidelines should be followed. Universal precautions for hand hygiene should be adhered to as this is an aseptic technique (NPSA, 2004). The most common site for obtaining a sample is the radial artery, but the brachial or femoral arteries can also be used should circulation in any of these areas be poor.

In an Intensive Therapy Unit (ITU), an arterial line may be used for frequent sampling but this can be prone to risks. Arterial stabs are usually performed on patients on a general respiratory ward. This can be painful for the patient and, if it has to be done frequently, it might be worth assessing the patient's condition and whether they need to be managed in an HDU (High Dependency Unit) or ITU.

As an alternative to the radial artery, arterialised capillary blood samples can be taken, usually from the ear lobe. This can be achieved by rubbing the earlobe with a vasodilator cream, ensuring a rapid flow of blood through the capillary. A small nick will allow blood to ooze out which can be collected in a fine capillary tube and analysed immediately, taking care not to introduce any air. It has been found that $PaCO_2$ results are within 0.1 kPa and pH is the same when compared to arterial blood (Zavorsky et al., 2007).

Management of respiratory failure

Although there are a number of options to consider when managing exacerbations of COPD and respiratory failure, the principles of the management of respiratory failure are the same:

- correct hypoxaemia
- reverse acidosis
- treatment of the underlying cause.

This can be achieved by the use of bronchodilators, corticosteroids, antibiotics, oxygen therapy and non-invasive ventilation.

Bronchodilators

Broncho-dilators

In an acute exacerbation the dose of bronchodilator should be increased. It is probable that the patient's inhaler technique is compromised when they are acutely breathless, and in these cases spacer devices can considerably improve deposition of drugs in the lung. If the patient is deemed to have sufficient inspiratory flow, dry-powder devices can also improve deposition. However, if the hospitalised patient is severely ill, it may be necessary to use a nebuliser.

The aim of treatment with nebulisers is to deliver a therapeutic dose of a drug in aerosol form within a short period of time, normally between five and ten minutes. In respiratory failure bronchodilators are given nebulised either via a face mask or mouthpiece depending on the drug. For example, anticholinergics are given via a mouthpiece due to potential side effects such as glaucoma.

In the hospital setting, piped oxygen is generally used to drive the nebulisers, but this is not recommended for patients with respiratory failure due to COPD as there is a high risk of developing or worsening hypercapnia. Nebulisers in this case should be driven by air and if the patient requires oxygen therapy they should be given oxygen via nasal cannula while the nebuliser is being used. It is important that the patient should be changed to hand-held inhalers as soon as their condition allows, as this may permit earlier discharge (NICE, 2004).

Corticosteroids

Cortico-steroids

Corticosteroids work by suppressing inflammation and hospitalised patients with an exacerbation of COPD should have a short course of oral steroids. Use of oral corticosteroids in this situation can result in faster improvement in lung function and shorter hospital stays (Davies *et al.*, 1999). It is important to remember that oral corticosteroids are not recommended for long-term use due to side effects and they should be stopped at the end of the prescribed course. Inhaled steroids have fewer side effects due to the lower dose that is required but there is no evidence to support the use in the acute situation.

Antibiotics

Antibiotics

There is no evidence to support the prophylactic use of antibiotics in stable COPD. During an exacerbation, if there is evidence of increased breathlessness and increased sputum volume or purulence then their use is recommended (NICE, 2004). The choice of antibiotic depends on the sensitivity of the infected sputum following microbiology or according to local antibiotic guidelines. Initial treatment options include aminopenicillin (e.g. amoxicillin), macrolide (e.g. erythromycin) and tetracycline. Seven days' treatment is usually sufficient.

Respiratory stimulants

Respiratory stimulants

Doxapram is the most commonly used respiratory stimulant in respiratory failure as it acts centrally to stimulate the respiratory drive. It must be given intravenously and is not recommended for long-term use as the side effects include tremor, sweating, confusion and agitation. NICE (2004) recommend its use when non-invasive ventilation (NIV) is unavailable or the inappropriate treatment for respiratory failure. NIV is the preferred option.

Oxygen therapy

Oxygen therapy in the acute situation

If a COPD patient is hypoxic it is important that they are given sufficient oxygen to correct their hypoxia. Giving too little oxygen will not correct hypoxia while giving oxygen in excessive concentrations can be dangerous for some patients. COPD should be managed using controlled oxygen therapy as there is a risk that uncontrolled oxygen therapy can result in the patient retaining CO_2 leading to the development of respiratory acidosis which can be fatal.

Some patients with COPD may have a permanently high level of CO_2 in their blood, and in those circumstances they may be relying on low oxygen levels to maintain their respiratory drive (McAllister, 2002). This is often referred to as hypoxic drive. If these patients are given too much supplementary oxygen some of them may hypoventilate and this can cause CO_2 levels to rise in the blood. The risks of this have been discussed earlier in this chapter. With this in mind the aim of oxygen therapy is to maintain adequate oxygenation (PaO_2 of more than 8 kPa) without worsening the hypercapnia.

If it is not possible to maintain an acceptable arterial oxygen level without causing an increase in CO_2 and a drop in arterial pH, NIV should be considered. In some cases, NIV may not be deemed appropriate, and then if the patient becomes progressively hypercapnic it may be possible to reduce oxygen therapy so that the patient's arterial gases are kept at the very minimum acceptable limit of 6.7 kPa.

Oxygen should be given via a Venturi mask and the concentration should be titrated according to arterial blood gas results, maintaining oxygen saturations (SpO_2) of between 88 and 92 per cent (MacNee & Rennard, 2004). It is not desirable to exceed SpO_2 of 93 per cent because there is no additional benefit but there may be an increased risk of hypercapnia. Importantly, to achieve adequate oxygenation it is not always sufficient to simply give patients 28 per cent oxygen, as responses to inhaled oxygen vary from patient to patient. Oxygen therapy should therefore be titrated to achieve adequate oxygenation and this may mean giving patients higher concentrations than 28 per cent. Clearly it is important to monitor the patient's response to oxygen therapy.

Unless in an emergency, oxygen therapy should be prescribed by an appropriately qualified practitioner and administered accordingly (Dodd, 2000). In one hospital survey it was found that 21 per cent of oxygen prescriptions were incorrectly written and 85 per cent of patients inadequately supervised. To ensure safe and effective oxygen treatment, the prescription should include flow rate/oxygen concentration, device, duration and monitoring of treatment (Bateman & Leach, 1998).

Patient concordance with oxygen therapy is important. The patient may be frightened and anxious; they are having difficulty in breathing and a mask over their face may be unwelcome. It helps to ensure the patient is in a comfortable position and that the mask is in the correct position to minimise the flow affecting the eyes.

Part of the treatment for respiratory failure is the continued use of nebulised bronchodilators. As stated previously patients who are hypercapnic and acidotic will benefit from the nebulisers being delivered by compressed air with supplementary oxygen being given via nasal cannula at a rate to maintain oxygen saturation between 90 and 92 per cent. Once completed, controlled oxygen therapy should be restarted (Murphy et al., 2001).

It has been recognised that when COPD patients in respiratory failure are travelling to hospital in an ambulance, the correct concentration of oxygen may not be given. The North West Oxygen Group researched this problem and the issue of oxygen therapy as a whole. The conclusion was that, as most ambulance journeys are less than 15 minutes, the risk of developing or worsening hypercapnia as a result of oxygen delivery was minimal for most patients provided that SpO_2 was maintained between 90 and 92 per cent (Murphy et al., 2001). In the pre-hospital stage diagnosis may be unclear and there is a greater risk of developing hypoxia than hypercapnia. The aim of the paramedics is to maintain oxygenation. This would be acceptable provided that the patient was fully assessed immediately on arrival at hospital and oxygen concentration requirements reflected the arterial blood gas analysis and not just oxygen saturation levels.

The North West Oxygen Group (Murphy et al., 2001) has developed guidelines on the oxygen management of COPD patients in the pre-hospital and emergency department setting. If the patient has hypoxic drive it is recommended that the patient is supplied with a card to alert paramedics and A&E staff to the normal oxygen saturation levels for that patient.

Monitoring oxygen therapy

Monitoring arterial blood gases, the depth and rate of respirations and SpO_2 will assess the effectiveness of treatment. On arrival at an emergency department immediate triage using blood gas analysis is important. Monitoring of respiratory rate and heart rate should be carried out every 15 minutes initially and pulse oximetry continuously. Arterial blood gases should be performed hourly, or more frequently if there is a clinical deterioration as an alternative treatment may need to be initiated (Murphy *et al.*, 2001). Accurate documentation is essential and this should be in line with local policy (Higgins, 2005).

If possible arterial blood gas analysis should be performed prior to starting oxygen therapy as this provides an accurate measurement of the effectiveness of treatment. FiO_2 (fraction of inspired oxygen) may need to be adjusted to reflect any changes in arterial blood gases, altering concentrations depending on the results. In patients with acute respiratory failure, continuous monitoring with pulse oximetry is also advised.

If there has been no improvement or there is deterioration in the patient's condition, another mode of treatment such as NIV should be considered. Frequently monitoring the patient will mean that the equipment required and informed consent can be obtained before an emergency situation arises.

Oxygen therapy should be stopped when the PaO_2 is more than 8 kPa and SaO_2 is more than 90 per cent when the patient is breathing in room air (Bateman & Leach, 1998). If a patient is being managed on long-term oxygen therapy this should be recommended unless otherwise indicated.

Controlled oxygen therapy and oxygen masks

Use of controlled oxygen concentration delivery for a COPD patient in acute respiratory failure is extremely important. Fixed performance systems such as the Venturi face mask deliver a fixed concentration of oxygen provided the oxygen flow rate is set at the correct level. Variable performance systems such as nasal cannula can deliver oxygen at a low flow rate but cannot give accurate concentrations. This is important if the patient requires a strictly controlled and accurate concentration of FiO_2. Another factor to be considered is the patient's breathing pattern. Depth, rate, and ventilatory minute volume (total volume of air breathed in and out in one minute) are important considerations.

Patients with COPD who are in acute respiratory failure do require a strictly controlled and accurate concentration of oxygen as too much oxygen can reduce the hypoxic drive and increase V/Q mismatching leading to CO_2 retention and a life-threatening respiratory acidosis. With this in mind it is worth describing some of the main types of oxygen masks and devices regularly used.

Low flow oxygen masks

These are simple masks and the concentration of oxygen depends on the patient's breathing rate and depth. With this device each breath taken is diluted by the air drawn in from the atmosphere and is variable because the patient's ventilatory minute volume varies with each breath. This mask is ideal for providing high concentrations of oxygen (40 to 60 per cent) from a flow rate of between six and ten litres per minute. Guidance on the suggested flow rate and the approximate concentration achieved is given by the manufacturer on the packaging (Porter-Jones, 2002).

With these masks it is difficult to achieve a low inspired oxygen concentration on a rate of less than five litres per minute due to rebreathing the exhaled gases. This occurs because exhaled air is not adequately flushed from the face mask. It is therefore not suitable for patients with type II respiratory failure who are already hypercapnic.

Nasal cannulae

These are a useful alternative if a patient is unable to tolerate a mask or finds it inconvenient as they are less claustrophobic and allow the patient to talk and eat without interruption of oxygen therapy, although blocked nasal passages will decrease the oxygen received. They are classed as low flow or variable devices as the exact FiO_2 is not known. This device can deliver an estimated oxygen concentration of between 24 and 40 per cent on a flow rate of one to four litres a minute. A flow rate above four litres a minute is very uncomfortable for the patient, resulting in dried mucous membranes and irritation.

Non-rebreathing mask

These masks have a one-way valve and have the advantage of providing a higher oxygen concentration than a low flow mask.

They are usually found in ambulances and in A&E. Also available are partial rebreathe masks that have no one-way valve only a reservoir bag. Again, FiO$_2$ varies depending on the patient's own breathing pattern and rate. To prevent the reservoir bag from collapsing on inspiration the flow should be sufficient, usually between 6 and 15 litres a minute, which will deliver 70 to 90 per cent.

High flow masks

These masks are able to deliver low concentrations of oxygen (24 to 35 per cent) accurately and will provide the total ventilatory requirement that is unaffected by the patient's breathing pattern. They also reduce the risk of CO$_2$ retention whilst improving hypoxaemia. Rebreathing of expired gas is not a problem as the mask is flushed by the high flow rates (Bateman & Leach, 1998).

The Venturi face mask is designed to mix air with the oxygen delivered in a set proportion, so that the concentration delivered is not dependent upon respiratory rate or tidal volume. The international colour-coded nozzles to fit onto face masks that deliver a fixed concentration of oxygen to the patient providing the flow rate is set at the correct level as specified by the manufacturer. Note that this is the minimum flow rate.

Another advantage for using a high flow Venturi device is that some patients are tachypnoeic and therefore will not feel comfortable with a low flow rate of oxygen. By increasing the flow – manufacturers provide a guide range for each concentration – the patient can be made to feel more comfortable by having a flow rate that reflects their respiratory rate. Making the patient more comfortable and less breathless will help in treatment compliance (Murphy *et al.*, 2001).

Venturi masks use the principle of jet mixing which means that when oxygen passes through a narrow orifice it produces a high velocity stream that draws a constant proportion of room air through the base of the Venturi valve. Air entrainment depends on the velocity of the jet (size of orifice and oxygen flow rate) and the size of the valve ports. It can be accurately controlled to give inspired oxygen levels of 24 to 60 per cent (Bateman & Leach, 1998). Some patients with COPD have reported that the sensation of dyspnoea is reduced by using a higher flow rate (Murphy *et al.*, 2001). Remember that increasing the flow rate above that recommended by the manufacturers does not increase the FiO_2 when using Venturi masks, however the minimum flow rate must be delivered to achieve an accurate concentration. Low flow oxygen masks do not provide the entire ventilatory requirement, though air is drawn in through the loose-fitting mask to supplement the oxygen flow rate.

Humidification

Whether to use humidification whilst administrating oxygen is debatable and local policies and guidelines should be followed. It is well known that oxygen can dry the mucous membranes causing soreness and can cause secretions to become stickier, making expectoration more difficult. However, at low flow rates, up to four litres a minute, there is sufficient natural humidification and, unless there are any contraindications, the patient should be encouraged to drink plenty of oral fluids.

A problem with humidification is that it can alter the oxygen concentration when delivered by a Venturi mask as the jet holes are affected by water vapour (Calianno, 1995). Sterile water should be used and changed daily to reduce the risk of infection.

Non-invasive ventilation (NIV)

Non-invasive ventilation

Occasionally the patient can become progressively hypercapnic and pH can drop even if oxygen is titrated so that PaO_2 is kept at a minimum acceptable level. In these cases NIV should be considered.

This section of the chapter is a basic introduction to the use of non-invasive ventilation as a modality of treatment for the COPD patient in acute respiratory failure. It is not intended on its own to equip a practitioner to provide NIV; further reading and education would be necessary. Individual ventilators will not be discussed as there are many on the market and each practitioner needs to be competent to use the machines available in their workplace.

Ventilatory support is the term used for respiratory support to a patient with the assistance of a mechanical ventilator which can be given in two ways:

- invasive ventilation – the upper airway is bypassed using an endotracheal tube or tracheostomy tube
- non-invasive ventilation (NIV) – support is given via the upper airway using a mask or similar device.

Randomised control trials have shown that NIV is a valuable treatment for acute type II respiratory failure. Its use avoids tracheal intubation with the associated risks and patients receiving this mode of treatment to do not need to be managed in an Intensive Treatment Unit. NIV can be initiated at an earlier stage of respiratory failure as the patient can be managed on general respiratory wards or high dependency unit depending on their clinical condition (BTS, 2002).

Research has also looked at the efficacy of non-invasive ventilation outside ITU. The results concluded that, if NIV was initiated at the appropriate time, conducted in an appropriately equipped and supervised environment, with protocols and guidelines then outcome is improved and mortality is reduced (Babu & Chauhan, 2003).

NIV is now widely used for the treatment of acute on chronic hypercapnic respiratory failure occurring with an exacerbation of COPD. Indeed NICE (2004) recommend that NIV should be used as treatment of choice for chronic hypercapnic patients during acute respiratory failure despite optimal medical therapy. Other recommendations include that wherever the treatment is delivered, staff should be trained and experienced in this mode of ventilation and are aware of its limitations. It is important to understand that most non-invasive ventilators will not ventilate the patient who is not making respiratory effort. These ventilators augment the patient's effort only. As discussed below, NIV is contraindicated in those patients who are not protecting their own airways.

NIV means the provision of ventilatory support by using a mask or similar device, called an 'interface'. There are some terms that a practitioner needs to be familiar with to help with understanding how NIV works and the benefits for the patient. The following list can be used as a guide.

Terminology associated with NIV

Terminology

CPAP	Continuous Positive Airway Pressure
PEEP	Positive End Expiratory Pressure
EPAP	Expiratory Positive Airway Pressure

IPAP	Inspiratory Positive Airway Pressure
Set rate	Minimum respiratory rate that the patient needs to achieve before the ventilator delivers a mandatory breath. In controlled or timed modes this would be the actual patient respiratory rate.
Ti	Time in inspiration
	For mandatory breaths the device determines the time the patient spends on inspiration.
RAMP	Period of time it takes the ventilator to reach the target prescribed pressure. For example, IPAP may be set at 16 cmH$_2$O, therefore the ventilator would start at 4 cmH$_2$O and gradually increase pressure until it reached the prescribed pressure in the time set.
Rise time	Time it takes the ventilator to reach inspiratory pressure. Altering the rise time can make a significant difference to the patient in terms of comfort and compliance by reducing or enhancing the flow delivery.

Modes used in NIV

A mode determines the level of interaction between the patient and the ventilatory therapy and how that therapy is delivered. Some modes allow the patient to breathe naturally and then the ventilator assists and enhances the patient's own effort. Other modes do not allow for patient interaction and will deliver a pre-set respiratory rate, pressure or volume. The availability of these modes depends on the ventilator model, therefore practitioners need to familiarise themselves with the workings of the ventilator being used. A comprehensive instruction manual is provided by the manufacturer for each.

Continuous positive airway pressure (CPAP)

This mode is used in acute or chronic hypoventilation to increase functional residual capacity helping to reduce the work of breathing in some patients and to increase PaO$_2$ to improve blood oxygenation. This mode delivers one continuous pressure throughout the breathing cycle. It is not unlike the sensation of putting your head out of a car window being driven down a motorway at speed; it does not mimic what happens in normal breathing.

CPAP is applied in type I respiratory failure. It is considered here in the context of the management of respiratory failure for completeness and to establish the rationale for using specific modes. This mode is not recommended for patients with COPD who need assistance during the inspiratory phase and expiratory phase of breathing (BTS, 2002).

Bi-level positive airway pressure

This is probably the most important mode where management of acute on chronic hypercapnic respiratory failure in COPD is concerned. BiPAP is one manufacturer's patented trade name for their bi-level mode of ventilators. This bi-level ventilation delivers a set pressure of air as the patient breathes in, called Inspiratory Positive Airways Pressure (IPAP), and a lower pressure on expiration called Expiratory Positive Airways Pressure (EPAP). Bi-level therefore alternates between IPAP and EPAP, synchronised with the patient's breathing pattern. In doing so it provides assistance during the inspiratory phase of respiration in the form of pressure support, and this helps improve tidal volume, reduces the work of breathing and therefore maximises the removal of CO_2 from the blood (Preston, 2001). This is important for a hypercapnic patient.

The pressure support provided by IPAP finishes at the start of the expiratory phase, which is when the ventilator begins to cycle to EPAP. But why would a patient need EPAP, which effectively means that they breathe out against a pressure that is generated by the ventilator? Remember that the COPD patient's airways can collapse. The delivery of EPAP effectively means that a positive pressure is maintained within the airways during the expiratory phase helping to inflate them and keep them and the alveoli open. On expiration many of the airways are therefore prevented from closing; they are 'splinted'. This increases the surface area for gaseous exchange, which leads to an increase in functional residual capacity and an increased PaO_2 and helps to reduce the work of breathing.

Spontaneous timed (S/T)

This mode delivers bi-level ventilation to the spontaneously breathing patient. IPAP and EPAP are determined by the clinician. However, if the patient's respiratory rate drops below a preset rate the ventilator will deliver a machine-triggered breath. In this mode a set rate or minimum breath rate is required as well as the length of time the patient is to be held at IPAP (time on inspiration or Ti).

Respiratory failure caused by exacerbations

For example, if the back-up breath rate is ten breaths a minute, the ventilator will check every six seconds and if the patient has not breathed in that time it will deliver a breath to the patient. Most ventilators have apnoea alarms to alert the clinician that the patient has stopped breathing.

Control or assist control

This mode controls ventilation and can be used in hypoventilating patients or those who have insufficient respiratory effort to either trigger the ventilator or maintain a sufficient time on inspiration. IPAP or pressure support is used to reduce the workload of breathing and improve tidal volume, therefore removing CO_2 retention. The set time on inspiration ensures that the patient receives adequate minute ventilation (respiratory rate x tidal volume).

Selection criteria for NIV

Criteria for NIV

At least two of the following should be present for NIV:

- moderate to severe acidosis (pH < 7.35)
- hypercapnia – $PaCO_2$ > 6.0 to 8.0 kPa (45–60 mmHg)
- respiratory rate > 25 breaths per minute
- moderate to severe dyspnoea with use of accessory muscles and paradoxical abdominal movement.

Exclusion criteria

If any of the following are present, NIV should not be employed:

- respiratory arrest
- cardiovascular instability (hypotension, arrhythmias, myocardial infarction)
- no gag reflex
- recent facial or gastrointestinal surgery
- craniofacial trauma, nasopharyngeal abnormalities
- facial burns
- undrained pneumothorax.

(BTS, 2002)

Not all patients are suitable for NIV but there is a high success rate for those who are able to have it (Plant & Elliott, 2003). Several factors predict the success of NIV in acute respiratory failure, these include a satisfactory interface between patient and mask, a rapid improvement in pH and less severe deterioration of pre-existing condition at the onset of treatment. Some factors that may predict success include an optimum treatment protocol, severity of acidosis on admission and location of therapy (Plant *et al.*, 2000). One important consideration is whether NIV is the ceiling of treatment or the patient should have mechanical ventilation if NIV fails? The BTS NIV guidelines (2002) highlight the need for local protocols in relation to exclusion criteria for initiating treatment and a treatment plan if NIV fails for any reason.

Interfaces

Interfaces

Using the wrong interface is one of the problems associated with NIV failure and so it is important to ensure that the correct mask is used (BTS, 2002). Masks come in a variety of sizes and can be full face, nasal pillows, nasal masks or those that cover the nose and mouth. Nasal masks or pillows offer the least invasive method, allowing the patient to talk, eat and drink at the same time as receiving assisted ventilation (Brigg, 1999). It is imperative that masks are correctly sized and fitted. The specific sizing gauge for any given mask should be used to ensure a correct fit. An ill-fitting and uncomfortable mask is one of the most frequently cited causes of patient non-compliance.

Masks are now made of silicone to provide an adequate seal between mask and patient. The skin, especially the bridge of the nose, is prone to breakdown due to continuous pressure and the head gear straps being too tight. It is recommended that a protective dressing is applied to the skin over the nasal bridge to prevent pressure sore formation and necrosis. A degree of leakage around the mask is common and modern machines and masks will compensate for even significant leaks. A degree of leak is preferable to applying too tight a mask. Air swallowing may occur with face masks and may even produce abdominal distension causing further difficulty in breathing due to increased intra-thoracic pressure. Oxygen can administered via the entrainment port on the mask.

Monitoring

Monitoring a patient on NIV depends on the location of therapy and their clinical status. Those who are managed in an ITU or HDU setting will most probably be monitored according to the guidelines in use. Pulse oximetry, arterial blood gas analysis and clinical assessment should be monitored to analyse the effective-ness of treatment. Assessment should include:

- chest wall movement
- coordination of respiratory effort with the ventilator (synchrony)
- use of accessory muscles
- respiratory rate
- heart rate
- patient comfort
- mental state.

(BTS, 2002)

Ventilator settings should be checked to ensure that the correct settings are being used as inappropriate settings lead to patient non-compliance, inadequate tidal volume or too low or too high pressures. Improvement in breathlessness should be seen within one to two hours and can be associated with an improvement in mental state.

Oxygen saturation should be monitored continuously for at least 24 hours after commencing NIV, maintaining saturation between 85 and 90 per cent (BTS, 2002). This non-invasive method of monitoring can give a quick reference to the patient's condition, although arterial blood gas analysis must also be performed prior to treatment to give a baseline measurement and repeated after an hour of treatment. Subsequent analysis should be performed approximately 20 minutes after any change in any ventilator setting or mode of treatment.

The pH is the best marker of the severity of the patient's condition and reflects deterioration or improvement of alveolar ventilation (Plant & Elliott, 2003). In addition, a lowering of the respiratory rate is an indication that there has been a reduction in the patient's work of breathing. Evidence suggests that the pH and respiratory rate are the most significant prognostic indicators for NIV success or failure in the first four hours following initiation of treatment (Plant *et al.*, 2000). Pressures are titrated according to arterial blood gases. Remember increasing IPAP should reduce CO_2 and EPAP and/or entraining oxygen will improve oxygenation.

Patients who are being managed in a ward setting need to be monitored closely so that those who are not responding to treatment can then be transferred to the ITU or HDU for further treatment, if NIV is not the ceiling of treatment. Invasive mechanical ventilation then needs to be initiated, as failure may lead to a delay in intubation and an increase in mortality (Plant *et al.*, 2001).

Patient care

Patient care

A high level of psychological care is required before and during NIV. The patient will be breathless and may be agitated due to hypoxia, although this will improve. It is imperative that good interpersonal and communication skills are used to establish the patient on NIV. The practitioner's approach and reassurance is key to initiating treatment.

An adequate explanation of the ventilator and its effects should be given and any fears expressed by the patient or family should be allayed. The practitioner needs to be able to spend uninterrupted time with the patient enabling the setting up of equipment on the patient to be a smooth and unrushed procedure which develops patient confidence in both the practitioner and the ventilator.

It is a good idea to allow the patient some control over when the mask is applied and headgear tightened. You are more likely to establish the patient on the system if you involve them in the process. This obviously depends on their general condition. For this reason the BTS NIV guidelines recommend that initiating pressures should start at:

- IPAP 10 cms H_2O
- EPAP 4 cms H_2O.

You will probably find that this is stated in your unit protocol.

At first the patient may find it difficult to keep the mask on for more than a minute or two. If the practitioner is with them, they can then build up the time on the ventilator and it has been shown that NIV is unlikely to be successful on a ward with a low nurse-to-patient ratio (Elliott, 2004). Involving members of the multi-disciplinary team, such as the physiotherapist, for optimising the positioning and chest clearance techniques can improve patient compliance and outcomes.

Withdrawal/weaning of treatment

In the early phase of treatment, the patient should be ventilated for as long as can be tolerated and clinically indicated, especially in the first 24 hours, or until there is a marked improvement in their condition (BTS, 2002). Breaks can then be taken for the administration of drugs, physiotherapy or meals.

Some patients decide themselves when to stop treatment but BTS guidelines recommend that weaning should start during the day, maintaining NIV during the night. They also suggest that the respiratory rate should be less than 24 breaths per minute, heart rate less than 110 beats per minute and a compensated pH of more than 7.35 (BTS, 2002).

If the patient's condition deteriorates dramatically, consideration should be taken as to whether to treat with invasive ventilation or palliatively. This is a sensitive situation and can be overcome by discussing these issues with the patient and their family prior to any exacerbations. A clear plan covering what to do if the patient's condition deteriorates and a clear ceiling of therapy should be agreed by all involved in the patient's care. This should help to ensure that the wishes of the patient are respected (NICE, 2004).

References

Babu, K. and Chauhan, A. (2003). Non-invasive ventilation in chronic obstructive pulmonary disease. *British Medical Journal*, **326**(7382), 177–178.

Bateman, N. and Leach, R. (1998). ABC of oxygen: Acute oxygen therapy. *British Medical Journal*, **317**, 798–801.

Brigg, C. (1999). The benefits of non-invasive ventilation and CPAP therapy. *British Journal of Nursing*, **8**(20), 1355–1361.

British Thoracic Society (BTS) (2002). Non-invasive ventilation in acute respiratory failure. British Thoracic Society Standards of Care Committee. *Thorax*, **57**, 192–211.

Callianno, C. (1995). Oxygen therapy. *Nursing*, **12**, 33–38.

Davies, L., Angus, R. and Calverley, P. (1999). Oral corticosteroids in patients admitted to hospital with exacerbations of Chronic Obstructive Pulmonary Disease: A prospective randomised controlled trial. *Lancet*, **354**, 456–460.

Dodd, M. (2000). Audit of oxygen prescribing before and after the introduction of a prescription chart. *British Medical Journal*, **321**, 864–865.

Elliott, M. (2004). Non-invasive ventilation for acute respiratory disease. *British Medical Bulletin*, **72**, 83–97.

Global Initiative for Chronic Obstructive Lung Disease (GOLD) (2006) *Global Strategy for the Diagnosis, Management and Prevention of Chronic Obstructive Pulmonary Disease*. Workshop Report November 2006. Bethesda: NLHBI/WHO.

Higgins, D. (2005). Oxygen therapy. *Nursing Times,* **101**(4), 30–31.

Lynes, D. (2003). An introduction to blood gas analysis. *Nursing Times*, **99**(54), 54–57.

Lynes, D. and Riches, A. (2003). Managing hypoxia and hypercapnia. *Nursing Times*, **99**(57), 58–60.

MacNee, W. and Rennard, S. (2004). *Fast Facts: Chronic Obstructive Airways Disease*. Oxford: Health Press.

McAllister, J. (2002). Special focus on chronic obstructive pulmonary disease. *Nursing Times*, **98**(41), 37–39.

Murphy, R., Mackway-Jones, K., Sammy, I., Driscoll, P., O'Driscoll, R., O'Reilly, J., Niven, R., Bentley, A., Brear, G. and Kishen, R. (2001). Emergency oxygen therapy for the breathless patient. Guidelines prepared by North West Oxygen Group. *Emergency Medicine Journal*, **18**, 421–423.

National Institute for Health and Clinical Excellence (NICE) (2004). Chronic Obstructive Pulmonary Disease: National clinical guideline on management of chronic obstructive pulmonary disease in adults in primary and secondary care. Guideline 12. *Thorax*, **59** (Suppl. 1), S1–S232.

National Patient Safety Agency (2004). Achieving our Aims: Evaluating the results of the pilot 'Clean Your Hands' campaign.
Available at www.npsa.nhs.uk/cleanyourhands, accessed 1.8.07.

Plant, P. and Elliott, M. (2003). Chronic Obstructive Pulmonary Disease 9: Management of ventilatory failure in COPD. *Thorax*, 58, 537–542.

Plant, P., Owen, J. and Elliott, M. (2000). Early use of non-invasive ventilation for acute exacerbations of Chronic Obstructive Pulmonary Disease on general respiratory wards: A multicentre randomised control trial. *Lancet*, 355, 1931–1935.

Plant, P., Owen, J. and Elliott, M. (2001). Non-invasive ventilation in acute exacerbations of Chronic Obstructive Pulmonary Disease: Long-term survival and predictors of in-hospital outcome. *Thorax*, 56, 708–712.

Porter-Jones, G. (2002). Short-term oxygen therapy. *Nursing Times*, 98(40), 53–56.

Preston, R. (2001). Introducing non-invasive positive pressure ventilation. *Nursing Standard*, 15(26), 42–45.

Scanlan, C., Wilkins, R. and Stoller, J. (1999). *Egan's Fundamentals of Respiratory Care*, 7th edn. St Louis: Mosby.

Woodrow, P. (2004). Arterial blood gas analysis. *Nursing Standard*, 18(21), 45–52.

Zavorsky, G., Cao, J., Mayo, N., Gabbay, R. and Murias, J. (2007). Arterial versus capillary blood gases: A meta-analysis. *Respiratory Physiology & Neurobiology*, 155(3), 268–279.

Chapter 8
Smoking and smoking cessation
Dave Burns

Cigarette consumption is the largest cause of premature mortality in the Western world, with ischaemic heart disease, cerebrovascular disease and lung cancer accounting for significant numbers of premature deaths. Parrot and Godfrey (2004) outline some of the economics of smoking cessation in the UK. These include: in the UK, approximately £1.5 billion a year is spent on treating smoking-related disease with £127 million spent on lung cancer alone; £410 million is spent treating children with disease related to passive smoking; in adults, passive smoking accounts for at least 1000 deaths annually.

They also point out that there are wider economic benefits in terms of reduction in illness from passive smoking, resulting in savings to both the employer and the NHS. In addition, non-smokers experience a better quality of life compared to smokers but this discrepancy reduces once smoking cessation occurs. From a COPD aspect, stopping smoking is seen as the only intervention to have a marked impact on the course of the disease, changing the clinical course of the disease by preserving lung function (Anzueto, 2006).

Epidemiologically the relationship between smoking and social class is a well-demonstrated one. Jarvis (2004) states that, among affluent men and women in the UK, the proportion of smokers who have quit has more than doubled since the early 1970s, from about 25 per cent to nearly 60 per cent, whereas in the poorest groups the proportion has remained at around ten per cent. Bancroft, Wiltshire *et al.* (2003) summarise research showing that in social class V, 45 per cent of males and 56 per cent of females smoke, compared to 12 per cent and 11 per cent respectively in social class I. Jarvis *et al.* (2003) investigated 'hardcore' smoking in the UK and identified 16 per cent of their sample as hardcore smokers. Employed in manual occupations, living in rented accommodation and having left education by the age of 16 were all features of many of those classed as hardcore, again demonstrating the correlation between smoking and socio-economic group.

Given these facts, numerous questions arise. Why do so many smokers carry on smoking? Why do so many individuals begin to smoke? More interestingly, why does cigarette smoking, with its massive impact on premature death, not seem to arouse the same intensity of debate as illegal drugs such as heroin and cocaine? There is a paradox in how legal drugs (cigarettes and alcohol) are viewed compared to illegal drugs, yet the psychosocial precursors to use of legal or illegal drugs, and their effects on neurophysiological function, are remarkably similar. In addition, the number of smoking-related deaths each year in the UK far outweigh those caused by, for example, heroin use. This suggests that tobacco control is a more important issue, at least in terms of 'direct health' consequences.

This chapter focuses on a number of areas and will begin by discussing the reasons why individuals decide to start smoking. This section will consider some of the social circumstances and psychological factors which influence individuals to start and the neurobiological mechanisms which may thwart some individuals' attempts to stop even after a relatively short smoking history. The ideal way to manage smoking-related diseases such as COPD would be to prevent individuals smoking in the first place and so developing some understanding of why smokers start is important. An important related aspect within this theme is the role of nicotine in developing and maintaining addiction.

A second major theme is the detrimental effect of smoking, including some discussion of smokers' perceptions of the advantages of smoking which may militate against interventions designed to stop them smoking. Linked to this is some discussion on the benefits of stopping smoking, both from a short-term physiological standpoint and a longer-term disease avoidance perspective. The final section will discuss the strategies to help individuals stop smoking and their relative efficacy.

Starting to smoke

Evidence concerning the initiation of smoking related to social class was provided by Sweeting and West (2001), who surveyed 2196 15-year-old females in West Scotland. While the definition of 'current smoker' did not differ significantly across social class, as the definition of current smoker became more stringent in terms of the amount and frequency of smoking, the number of smokers from households in lower socio-economic groups rose markedly.

Psychological factors

Intermingled with these social factors are psychological factors which explain why people start and continue to smoke. Reasons for uptake of smoking in teenagers are usually given as rebellion, peer pressure or wanting to conform. Rugåsa *et al.* (2001) interviewed 85 10- to 11-year olds from economically-deprived areas of Northern Ireland in some depth about smoking and tobacco addiction. The children in this study seemed to differentiate between childhood and adult smoking. Adults were viewed as smoking in order to cope with their lives and viewed as addicted and this addiction seemed to differentiate them from child smokers, who were seen as smoking in order to 'be cool' or to gain group membership. Smoking in children was seen more as a social issue and something that was done to aid functioning.

A relatively early study by Tucker (1984) attempted to distinguish 'intenders' (to smoke) from 'non-intenders'. He assessed 335 adolescent Americans using validated personality and self-esteem tools. Findings revealed seven major personality variables which were different between the two groups. Non-intenders had higher self-esteem, were more self-confident, moralistic, confident, group-oriented, conservative and tender-minded than intenders, who in turn were more liberal, apprehensive and self-sufficient than non-intenders.

West *et al.* (1999) observed that, while early teenage years were clearly identified as the prime time to start smoking, there is a considerable discrepancy between adult smokers and those who start at school. A considerable portion of smokers do, therefore, start later in life. West *et al.* carried out a longitudinal study of 1009 15-year-old schoolchildren, who were followed up at 16, 18, 21 and 23 years of age. Smoking was assessed initially along with parental and sibling smoking and social class. The investigators found that smoking rates more than doubled between the ages of 15 and 23, rising from 14 per cent to 36 per cent. A key finding was that the likelihood of subjects starting to smoke between the ages of 18 and 21 was increased threefold if they had a friend who smoked.

A common reason for smoking is stress reduction, yet it is unclear whether exposure to stress leads to a decision to start smoking. Byrne *et al.* (1995) investigated this issue, interviewing over 6000 students at baseline and one year later when stress levels were assessed. Respondents were classified as non-smokers at baseline follow-up; non-smokers at baseline but regular smokers at follow-up; and regular smokers at baseline and follow-up. Overall, non-smokers had significantly lower stress scores than the other two groups. In addition, smokers had more stress in school and family environments.

Women and smoking

Byrne *et al.* also observed that more girls started smoking than boys. This is particularly relevant because, while there is evidence that, worldwide, males are successfully stopping smoking, females are not so successful, and, in the context of the current discussion, more females are starting to smoke than males.

As an illustration of this point, Mackay and Amos (2003) state that about 200 million women in the world smoke, with 22 per cent of these living in developed countries. They further argue that, as more women are starting to smoke, the total number of women smoking in the world by 2025 could be 532 million. The authors argue that, while the global tobacco epidemic amongst men is declining, in women it will not reach its peak until well into the 21st century. Driving factors in this include changes in socio-cultural behaviour, increased spending power among females and greater difficulty in quitting among women.

Smoking on film and television

A further influence on the decision to start smoking is exposure to smoking in films. Sargent *et al.* (2001) argued that little attention had been paid to media influences on the decision to start smoking; as evidence suggests that the typical American adolescent watches two to three hours of television daily, and approximately two to three films a week, they felt that this was worth investigating. The investigators found a strong relationship between the number of films watched and smoking attempts (see Table 8.1).

Table 8.1

Watching smoking in films and attempting smoking

Number of smoking incidences observed	Percentage attempting smoking
0–50	4.9
51–100	13.7
101–150	22.1
> 150	31.3

(Sargent *et al.*, 2001)

What might explain this finding? Dozier *et al.* (2005) analysed the content of the one hundred top grossing films in 2002 in terms of the number of smoking occurrences, the characteristics of the smokers, and the portrayal of the consequences of smoking. They found that: six per cent of the characters smoked in 453 incidents; smokers tended to be major characters, usually placed in leadership roles and portrayed as 'elite' in that they were white, male and mature; and that only 0.4 per cent of tobacco incidences resulted in death, despite the fact that smoking is the biggest worldwide cause of premature death. These findings indicate that smoking on film is portrayed as glamorous and as having no detrimental effects.

Gutschoven and Bulck (2004) examined the relationship between smoking and watching television amongst Belgian schoolchildren. They found that subjects who watched more than five hours television a week smoked between 60 and 147 more cigarettes a week than those subjects watching less than one hour's television a week. These studies then point to a definite media influence on both the experimentation with cigarette smoking (presumably due to some role-modelling influence) and the volume of cigarettes smoked.

Conclusions

Overall, there is evidence to support the notion that smoking initiation and prevalence is a function of social class, with increased smoking behaviour becoming more prevalent in social classes IV and V.

It is clear that there are a number of mechanisms and circumstances driving the initiation. Some appear to be related to role modelling by parents and older siblings, although the mass media, certainly films and television, also seem to play a part. Stress may be a factor because of, for example, lifestyle limitations. The evidence presented would seem to indicate that more confident individuals seem less likely to intend to smoke, or even experiment, and this may indicate that they possess better coping strategies.

Pressure to conform may play a large part in initiation, especially where the subject of the pressure is from a family who smoke and where smoking may be the norm. The role of personality is unclear, with smokers depicted in some studies by either non-smokers, or their smoking peers, as sensation-seeking or non-conformist, while other evidence suggests that those more likely to smoke may be shy, depressed or experiencing stress. Patently, there are many different factors operating in many different contexts.

Time to addiction and biological factors

Time to addiction

Having considered why people start smoking, a further important issue is the time it takes to become addicted. An interesting study was carried out by DiFranza *et al.* (2002). This was a prospective and retrospective study examining details of tobacco use in 679 school pupils aged 12 to 13. The investigators were interested in tobacco use (including frequency and amount of use), attempts to quit and development of symptoms of dependence. Pupils were interviewed on eight occasions over the study period, using validated psychological measures of nicotine dependence, and were asked to complete 'smoking diaries' which were then used to assess their nicotine intake. They were further asked about attempts to quit, and success or relapse.

Of the 332 subjects who had used tobacco, 40 per cent reported symptoms of dependence, with a median latency of 21 days for girls and 183 days for boys. The median frequency of tobacco use at the onset of dependence symptoms was two cigarettes, one day per week. Thus, as the authors conclude, dependence develops rapidly after the onset of intermittent smoking and, worryingly, there does not appear to be a minimum nicotine intake for symptoms of dependence to appear.

What about biological factors in nicotine addiction? Nicotine is capable of producing feelings of pleasure and reward by stimulation of an area in the brain called the meso limbic system. Crucial to the activity of this centre is the indirect or direct stimulation of neurones within it by nicotine. Nicotine binds to a receptor termed the nicotinic Acetylcholine receptor (nAChR) which comprises five subunits identified as β, ε, γ, α and δ. Of interest in nicotine addiction are the α (alpha) and β (beta) subunits, as these form the nAChRs found within the central nervous system and more specifically within the dopaminergic pathways associated with reward and addiction.

Recent evidence (Tapper *et al.*, 2004) has pointed to the pivotal importance of the $\alpha 4$ subunit in the development of addiction to nicotine.

The investigators showed that genetically-engineered mice with predominantly $\alpha 4$ nAChRs showed much more nicotine-induced neuronal activity, even at extremely low nicotine concentrations showed greater response to nicotine administration in terms of increase in the numbers of nAChRs and developed nicotine tolerance in a very short space of time. The authors therefore conclude that activation of $\alpha 4$ receptors is sufficient for nicotine-induced reward, tolerance and sensitisation. This might offer some insight as to why some individuals find quitting easy, while others have marked difficulties due to differences in nAChR composition which drive the addiction more strongly in those individuals. Nicotine addiction is a 'physiological' problem and one that arguably deserves a more sympathetic hearing than it receives.

The consequences of cigarette smoking

Consequences of smoking

The dangers associated with smoking had been suspected for many years. However, it took until the late 20th century to demonstrate them precisely. Doll and Peto (1976) published a landmark study in 1976 showing the consequences of smoking on health. It followed the smoking habits and mortality of more than 35,000 British GPs over a 30-year period and demonstrated a clear correlation between smoking and leading causes of death such as cardiovascular, cerebrovascular and pulmonary disease.

The most common manifestation of pulmonary disease related to cigarette smoking is COPD. Here, inflammatory mediators secreted by white cells attracted to the lungs by cigarette smoke damage the lung structure irreversibly. Lung function is progressively lost at approximately twice the rate for a non-smoker, with susceptible individuals who continue to smoke eventually becoming respiratory cripples, housebound and heavily dependent on others for help in many cases. The commonly-quoted estimate is that while only about 20 per cent of smokers will develop COPD, 90 per cent of COPD sufferers will have a significant smoking history. However, a recent study by Løkke *et al.* (2006) has found that a more accurate figure for susceptibility is at least 25 per cent. Interestingly, similar figures apply to lung cancer both in terms of the population of smokers at risk and the smoking history of those developing the condition.

In view of the above, it would seem logical to not smoke at all, or to quit as soon as possible. General benefits of stopping smoking outlined by Jenkins (2004) include: a reduction in risk of coronary heart disease within one year of 50 per cent compared to that of continuing smokers and a subsequent return to the risk level of a non-smoker after 15 years; a 50 per cent reduction in the risk of ear, nose, throat and oesophageal cancers within five years, and a 50 per cent reduction in lung cancer risk within ten years. Jenkins indicates other benefits such as a saving of £1,500 per year for a 20-a-day smoker, reduced risk of passive disease to others and improvements in smell and taste within days.

With regard to respiratory aspects, Willemse *et al.* (2004) performed an exhaustive review of studies examining the effects of smoking cessation on respiratory symptoms, lung function, airway hyper-responsiveness and inflammation. Some of the major findings were:

- a reduction in episodic respiratory symptoms such as cough and dyspnoea
- a reduction in the fall of FEV_1 in patients with and without chronic symptoms
- normalisation of the fall of FEV_1 in all stages of COPD.

Smoking cessation

Unfortunately quitting is difficult. Approximately 70 per cent of smokers try to quit each year, with only approximately two per cent succeeding. Even here there are problems. However quitting is defined, relapse is a common feature and one very relevant to the concept of addiction. As an illustration of this, an early study by Davison and Duffy (1982) examined smoking habits of 52 patients who had survived for more than five years after being diagnosed with lung cancer. Of these, 56 per cent had stopped smoking before the operation, while no patients smoked in the immediate post-operative period. However, 48 per cent became regular smokers again, usually within one year of the operation.

Why then does smoking cessation appear to be so unsuccessful? There are a number of issues here. Very broadly, they include:

- reluctance of smokers to consider giving up (including barriers and perceived benefits)
- the part family members might play in influencing the decision to quit
- the role played by healthcare professionals.

One theoretical framework which lends itself to either the decision to start smoking or attempts to stop at some point is the Health Belief Model (HBM) (Rosenstock, 1974). This model proposes that the decision to start smoking, or perhaps to stop smoking, is based around a number of variables. These include demographics such as: age, gender and social class; cues individuals may pick up from the mass media; the perceived risk of developing a smoking-related disease, e.g. lung cancer; the perceived severity of that disease; the benefits of performing a behaviour such as stopping smoking; and the barriers to that behaviour.

Price and Everett (1994) interviewed 500 economically-disadvantaged residents in Ohio and used the HBM as a basis for their investigation. Thinking about the variables within the HBM reveals a number of possible explanations for starting to smoke. Demographic factors such as age, gender and social class have already been discussed. In terms of the benefits and barriers as components of the HBM, Price and Everett (1994) found that almost 90 per cent of their respondents identified saving money, living longer, feeling healthier and avoiding hassles in public places were benefits. Conversely, 70 per cent on average felt that it was hard to give up smoking because: it was a habit; it helped them relax; it stopped them from being bored; tobacco was addictive; and many friends of smokers were smokers themselves. Many of these points were also found in work by Amos *et al.* (2006).

In addition, more than 70 per cent of respondents in the Price and Everett study were aware that passive smoking and air pollution were lung cancer risk factors but 41 per cent believed that there was nothing that people could do to prevent lung cancer, despite the fact that overall 89 per cent agreed with the statement 'If I smoke cigarettes I am more likely to develop lung cancer'. In addition, 83 per cent were overly optimistic about the potential of chest X-rays to help save the life of a lung cancer patient. This is far from the truth, with approximately 90 per cent of those diagnosed dying within one year. This study revealed some interesting views, albeit some which appeared to be totally contradictory.

Another reason for not wanting to give up could be denial of the harmful effects of smoking. Dissonance theory (Festinger, 1957) proposes that where our actions do not correlate with what we know, a state of tension or 'cognitive dissonance' exists. To reduce this tension we must change either our actions (e.g. stop smoking) or else revise our views. For the first of these, stopping smoking is difficult. Jenkins (2004) states that of the 30 per cent of smokers trying to quit at any time, only two to three per cent will be successful.

In relation to the biology of addiction, Kozlowski *et al.* (1989) interviewed smoking individuals who were addicted to drugs such as alcohol, benzodiazepines, heroin, or cocaine and receiving treatment at an addiction centre. Overall, most of the interviewees rated the pleasure derived from cigarettes compared to their other drug as significantly less, thought that giving up their drug would be easier than giving up cigarettes and craved cigarettes more than their drug, despite experiencing less pleasure from cigarettes. This survey illustrates some of the anomalies we face in terms of our thinking about nicotine addiction and shows how addictive cigarettes can be.

Within the context of dissonance theory, if we cannot stop smoking, then tension must be reduced by modifying our attitudes towards cigarettes, using for example the scenario of a family member who smoked 40 a day and lived to the age of 90 before being killed in a freak accident. The problem here is that family members like this, although very rare, do represent reality to the patient, and so help justify them in carrying on smoking. Other examples of how to reduce dissonance might include the knowledge that healthcare professionals smoke (and therefore it can't be that bad) or the mistaken belief that lung cancer is easily treated and that it will be enough for them to stop smoking when they get it.

A psychological concept which has evoked much interest with regard to smoking cessation is the Transtheoretical Model, commonly referred to as the 'Stages of Change Model' (Prochaska & Di Clemente, 1983). This is based around the idea that individuals move through five stages when making a change in their health behaviour. These are the pre-contemplative stage, the contemplative stage, the preparation stage, the action stage and the maintenance stage. In concrete terms, individuals at the precontemplative stage are not even considering, for example, stopping smoking; those at the contemplative stage may have thought about it, perhaps because of something they have seen or read; in the preparation stage they are getting ready to implement the change (for example setting their quit date once they have started taking Buproprion); the action stage involves them stopping smoking and putting into practice techniques such as avoidance and distraction, in addition to taking prescribed medication; and the maintenance stage involves adhering to their decision not to smoke.

While commonly referred to in the literature on smoking cessation, the model does not explore the reasons for, for example, stopping smoking, or the resources available and seems simply to indicate a set of logical steps that smokers may pass through. West and Sohal (2006) in discussing this model criticise it on a number of counts, including asserting that it is not applicable to many people. West and Sohal argue that, for many people, a 'catastrophic' pathway leads to a decision to stop smoking. They surveyed almost 1000 smokers and showed that this was the case, with up to 50 per cent of quit attempts being made spontaneously. Interestingly, those quitting spontaneously were more likely to succeed compared to those planning to quit.

Further evidence to support the idea of spontaneous quitting was provided by Stanton *et al.* (1999) who interviewed out-of-school youth smokers and found that only 52 per cent were 'contemplating' quitting. One study (Scott Lennox *et al.*, 1998) evaluated the impact of a one-day training session in the use of the Stages of Change model for primary healthcare teams in terms of patients' recall of health professionals' behaviour, and on smoking outcomes in patients, and found no significant effects in terms of using the model to increase smoking cessation rates.

Strategies to stop smoking

Strategies to stop smoking

If smokers do have insight into the potential harm they are doing (and published and anecdotal evidence suggests that they do), why are so many people still smoking? Undoubtedly quitting is difficult, but it can be done. However, accurately gaining a picture of successful quit rates is problematic. This is partly due to difficulties in defining what constitutes successful quitting in terms of the period of abstinence and the most accurate method of ascertaining that quitting has actually taken place.

Some data are available, however. Jenkins (2004) points out that 70 per cent of smokers want to stop, with 30 per cent trying at any one time. However success rates are poor at 3 to 6 per cent, with 60 per cent of those relapsing doing so at two weeks.

Data from the NHS stop smoking services published by Medical News Today (2004) showed that during the period April to September 2003 almost 130,000 people had set a quit date through the stop smoking services. At four week follow-up, just over 50 per cent had successfully quit. Success rates were higher in the over 60s (63 per cent) compared to those under 18 (39 per cent). However, this was based on self report and represents a very short time period associated with successful quitting.

Lancaster *et al.* (2006) indicate that many people return to smoking within one year, but do not give a precise figure. This would suggest that the four week criterion used by the NHS stop smoking services is generous in the extreme. In addition, Jenkins supports the point made earlier that success in quitting appears to be a function of social class, with higher success rates in higher socio-economic groups.

Psychosocial interventions

While there is a large body of evidence supporting the efficacy of the various conventional treatments, it is apparent that a substantial number of smokers (30 per cent) will not attempt to give up at all. Roddy *et al.* (2006) investigated the barriers and motivators to smoking cessation among smokers from socially-deprived groups. They comment that smokers from lower socio-economic groups are just as likely to want to quit as smokers from higher socio-economic groups, but have greater difficulty because of perceived low self-efficacy (they do not believe they have the ability to stop smoking). They carried out focus group interviews with 39 smokers who had all attempted to stop smoking within the last year without utilising local smoking cessation services and failed, with the aim of identifying barriers and motivators. Results were interesting in that perceived barriers included fear of being judged, fear of failing, a lack of knowledge about existing services, a perception that treatments such as nicotine replacement therapy (NRT) were both expensive and ineffective and negative perceptions of Buproprion based on media reporting.

The motivational factors in this study included: a personalised, non-judgemental approach, combining counselling with affordable pharmacological interventions; a convenient and flexible time of service delivery; and the possibility of subsidised complementary therapies.

The psychosocial and biological factors driving nicotine addiction would seem to warrant both psychosocial and biological (pharmacological) interventions to assist smokers to quit. There are a number of interventions available to help smoking cessation, including complementary therapies. Of all these the two most extensively studied and evidence-based are psychosocial support and, in terms of pharmacotherapy, NRT and Buproprion. It may be that smokers attempting to quit (and perhaps healthcare professionals prescribing these therapies) overrely on the pharmacological interventions. However, most research, and indeed guidelines, on smoking cessation make the point that the most successful interventions are those combining both psychosocial and pharmacological interventions.

The power of basic advice

This idea is emphasised by Coleman (2004), who states that these two interventions contribute about equally to the successful cessation of smoking. Coleman further argues that the success rate of 'brief advice' (defined as advice lasting two to three minutes) on quitting is about 1 in 40 smokers – making this one of the most cost-effective interventions in medicine. Coleman argues that behavioural support which is carried out outside routine clinical care by appropriately-trained counsellors is the most effective non-pharmacological intervention for those smokers who are strongly motivated to quit. In support of this argument, a study by Willemse *et al.* (2005) examined the effect of an intensive smoking cessation support programme without pharmacological support and found quit rates at one year of 42 per cent in patients with COPD or bronchitis and 68 per cent in healthy subjects. This involved 15 group meetings, so there may be issues about cost effectiveness but the study does reinforce the role of support in smoking cessation.

Perhaps the implication overall is that all healthcare professionals, regardless of the setting they work in, should at least be prepared to broach the topic of smoking with patients, deliver the message that it is harmful and be prepared to follow up patients who are attempting to quit. There is an important role here for secondary care staff, who, while not prescribing or being involved in smoking cessation programmes generally, should still ask about smoking in their patients and at least 'plant the seed' by providing brief advice and supporting this with written information. Secondary care staff could also provide extra support/reinforcement/advice to those patients who may have tried and failed previously. Simple comments such as 'But did you know that many people fail, some as much as six times, but still manage to quit eventually? So don't give up, you'll get there' are supportive, non-judgemental and informative. Information in hospital does not have to be detailed or time-consuming. While evidence for this idea does not appear to exist, it seems likely that if patients hear the same message from different clinicians in different settings time after time they may come to accept that they can succeed after all.

Smoking and smoking cessation

Raising the issue

How then should we approach the topic of smoking cessation with our patients? There is some evidence that healthcare professionals 'shy away' from this topic for different reasons, such as lack of confidence or a perception that they lack the necessary skills. Some may assume incorrectly that no smoking patient wants to be asked about their smoking; others assume that patients have 'heard it all before' and that they (as healthcare professionals) are wasting their time. However, the process of ascertaining where patients are in relation to smoking cessation can be very simple. Jenkins (2004) advocates a three question approach to smoking cessation.

- Do you smoke?
- Would you like to stop?
- Would you like my help to stop smoking? (There are treatments available.)

These correspond quite well with another well recognised approach – the five 'A's.

- Ask about smoking.
- Advise about the dangers.
- Assess willingness to stop.
- Assist in stopping.
- Arrange follow-up.

Where patients are motivated to quit, further brief assessment is useful. Identifying reasons for smoking, amount smoked per day, and patterns of smoking may all provide information which may guide the advice or counselling that the healthcare professional gives. In addition, identifying forthcoming 'stressors' such as moving house, changing job or attending for interview may help set an appropriate quit date. These events could impact negatively on the individual's attempt to quit and so quit attempts are better carried out in periods of personal and social stability.

Further resources to aid quitting can also be identified at assessment, be they enlisting the support of a spouse or partner (particularly where they also smoke), informing family, friends and colleagues of the impending quit date or choosing a jar to put the money into that is saved by not buying cigarettes. For some patients (probably a considerable number) it will not be their first attempt. (Some data indicates that up to six attempts are made before success is achieved.) These patients need to be reassured that first time success is not the norm and also be praised for 'climbing back on'. Identifying why they failed may also be useful, as this can be a learning tool for the patient.

Pharmacotherapy

Pharmaco-therapy

In terms of pharmacotherapy, the two most tried and tested interventions are NRT and Buproprion. The National Institute for Health and Clinical Excellence (NICE) guidelines advise that either of these therapies will double the chances of successful quitting compared to will power alone. NRT is available in a number of strengths and formulations including patches, lozenges and sprays. The dose and route of administration will vary and this will in turn be influenced by the patient's level of cigarette consumption. The maximum length of treatment is three to six months, again depending on the method of delivery.

Buproprion is available as tablets in one dose. Patients start on one tablet daily for six days prior to their identified quit date, before increasing to two tablets daily for the remainder of the treatment period, which for Buproprion should not exceed seven to nine weeks. Whichever treatment is used, patients should be provided with enough for two weeks. They should then be reviewed and repeat prescriptions issued only if they appear to be making genuine attempts to quit.

While both treatments are relatively safe, there is some risk of seizures in susceptible individuals taking Buproprion and patients being considered for this treatment need careful assessment. In addition, the drug is not recommended for use in under 16s, in pregnancy or during breast-feeding. Similar conditions apply to NRT. As a note of caution, NRT is contraindicated in severe cardiovascular disease although this may be used where non-pharmacological interventions in pregnancy have been unsuccessful.

More recently, a third pharmacological intervention has become available. This is Champix (varenicline), an $\alpha4\beta2$ antagonist. Like Buproprion it is taken in tablet form, although for the longer time of 12 weeks. Again patients need to set a quit date and commence therapy one week before this date. In the UK, NICE issued draft guidance on 31 May 2007 recommending that varenicline be available on NHS prescription.

While there are many studies examining the efficacy of these treatments they are, as stated, very effective overall. Wu *et al.* (2006) performed a meta-analysis of pharmacological therapies for smoking cessation showing overall that all therapies were effective; the most effective was the newest (varenicline). They do, however, comment that more studies may be required to consolidate this early finding. Where patients fail, a second attempt date needs to be considered carefully, along with policy restrictions on, for example, funding a second course of NRT.

Conclusion

There are many reasons why individuals start to smoke. It would make sense to target young people and prevent them smoking in the first place, but unfortunately this strategy seems to have little impact when smoking rates in teenagers are examined.

While psychosocial forces seem to be the predominant factor driving the intention to start smoking, evidence suggests that symptoms of dependency occur very quickly and at very low doses of nicotine consumption, illustrating the point that biological factors quickly help to maintain the addiction. Psychological theories may help us understand why smokers prefer to carry on smoking, although approximately 70 per cent of smokers do want to stop.

Success in smoking cessation is achieved by a combination of psychosocial support and pharmacological intervention using either NRT, Buproprion, or from 2007, varenicline. Smoking cessation is a highly cost-effective intervention in terms of actual cost, lives saved and quality of life improvements in sustained quitters. All healthcare professionals need to ask patients about smoking at every opportunity, provide brief advice in a friendly, non-judgemental manner, offer assistance in some way and, perhaps most importantly, realise that nicotine is highly addictive and quitting is not easy.

With good professional support many patients can quit and in doing so greatly improve their life expectancy, enhance the quality of the rest of their lives, reduce the risk of passive smoking-related diseases to those around them and save the NHS considerable sums of money.

References

Amos, A., Wiltshire, S., Haw, S. and McNeill, A. (2006). Ambivalence and uncertainty: Experiences of and attitudes towards addiction and smoking cessation in the mid-to-late teens. *Health Education Research*, **21**(2), 181–191.

Anzueto, A. (2006). Clinical course of Chronic Obstructive Pulmonary Disease: Review of therapeutic options. *American Journal of Medicine*, 119 (Suppl. A), S46–S53.

Bancroft, A., Wiltshire, J., Parry, O. and Amos, A. (2003). 'It's like an addiction first thing…afterwards it's like a habit': Daily smoking behaviour among people living in areas of deprivation. *Social Science & Medicine*, 56, 1261–1267.

Byrne, D., Byrne, A. and Reinhart, M. (1995). Personality, stress and the decision to commence cigarette smoking in adolescence. *Journal of Psychosomatic Research*, 39(1), 53–62.

Coleman, T. (2004). Use of simple advice and behavioural support. *British Medical Journal*, **328**, 397–399.

Corrigal, W. (1991). Understanding brain mechanisms in nicotine reinforcement. *British Journal of Addiction*, 86, 507–510.

Corrigal, W., Coen, K. and Adamson, K. (1994). Self-administered nicotine activates the mesolimbic dopamine system through the ventral tegmental area. *Brain Research*, **653**, 278–284.

Dani, J. and Biasi, M. (2001). Cellular mechanisms of nicotine addiction. *Pharmacology, Biochemistry & Behaviour*, **70**, 439–446.

Dani, J., Daoyun, J. and Zhou, F. (2001). Synaptic plasticity and nicotine addiction. *Neuron*, 31, 349–352.

Davison, G. and Duffy, M. (1982). Smoking habits of long-term survivors of surgery for lung cancer. *Thorax*, **37**, 331–333.

DiFranza, J., Savageau, J., Rigotti, N., Fletcher, K., Ockene, J. and McNeill, A. (2002). Development of symptoms of tobacco dependence in youths: 30-month follow-up data from the DANDY study. *Tobacco Control*, 11, 228–235.

Doll and Peto (1976). Mortality in reation to smoking: 20 years observations on male British doctors. *British Medical Journal* 1976, **2**, 1525–36

Dozier, D., Lauzen, M., Day, C., Payne, J. and Tafoya, M. (2005). Leaders and elites: Portrayals of smoking in popular films. *Tobacco Control*, 14, 7–9.

Festinger, L. (1957). *A Theory of Cognitive Dissonance*. Stanford, CA: Stanford University Press.

Gutschoven, K. and Bulck, J. (2004). Television viewing and smoking volume in adolescent smokers: A cross-sectional study. *Preventative Medicine*, 39, 1093–1098.

Jarvis, M. (2004). Why people smoke. *British Medical Journal*, **328**, 277–279.

Jarvis, M., Wardle, J., Owen, L. and Waller, J. (2003). Prevalence of hardcore smoking in England and associated attitudes and beliefs: Cross-sectional study. *British Medical Journal*, 326, 1061–1062.

Jenkins, G. (2004). What really works? *Practice Nurse*, 28(7), 52–58.

Kozlowski, L., Wilkinson, D., Skinner, W., Kent, C., Franklin, T. and Pope, M. (1989). Comparing tobacco cigarette dependence with other drug dependencies. *Journal of the American Medical Association*, 261, 898–907.

Lancaster, T., Hajek, P., Stead, L., West, R. and Jarvis, M. (2006). Prevention of relapse after quitting smoking: A systematic review of trials. *Archives of Internal Medicine*, 166(8), 828–835.

Løkke, A., Lange, P., Scharling, H., Fabricius, P. and Vestbo, J. (2006). Developing COPD: A 25 year follow-up study of the general population. *Thorax*, 61, 935–939.

Lucas, K. and Lloyd, B. (1999). Starting smoking: Girls' explanations of the influence of peers. *Journal of Adolescence*, 22, 647–655.

Mackay, J. and Amos, A. (2003). Women and tobacco. *Respirology*, 8(2), 123–130.

Medical News Today (2004). Health effects of smoking are more dangerous than thought. Available at http://www.medicalnewstoday.com, accessed 8.1.07.

Parrot, S. and Godfrey, C. (2004). Economics of cigarette smoking. *British Medical Journal*, 328, 947–949.

Price, J. and Everett, S. (1994). Perceptions of lung cancer and smoking in an economically disadvantaged population. *Journal of Community Health*, 19(5), 361–375.

Prochaska, J. and Di Clemente, C. (1983). Stages and processes of self change of smoking: Towards an integrative model of change. *Journal of Consulting Clinical Psychology*, 51(3), 390–395.

Roddy, E., Antoniak, M., Britton, J., Molyneux, A. and Lewis, S. (2006). Barriers and motivators to accessing smoking cessation services amongst deprived smokers: A qualitative study. *BMC Health Services Research*, 6, 147.

Rosenstock, J. (1974). The health belief model and preventive behaviour. *Health Education Monographs*, 2(4), 355–385.

Rugåsa, J., Knox, B., Sittlington, J., Kennedy, O., Treacy, M. and Abaunza, P. (2001). Anxious adults vs. cool children: Childrens' views on smoking and addiction. *Social Science & Medicine*, 53, 593–602.

Sargent, J., Beach, M., Dalton, M., Mott, L., Tickle, J., Ahrens, M. and Heatherton, T. (2001). Effect of seeing tobacco use in films on trying cigarette smoking in adolescents: Cross-sectional study. *British Medical Journal*, 323, 1–6.

Scott Lennox, A., Bain, N., Taylor, R., McKie, L., Donnan, P. and Groves, J. (1998). Stages of change training for opportunistic smoking intervention by primary healthcare team. Part 1: Randomised controlled trial of the effect of training on patient smoking outcomes and health professional behaviour as recalled by patients. *Health Education Journal*, 57, 140–149.

Snow, P. and Bruce, D. (2003). Cigarette smoking in teenage girls: Exploring the role of peer reputation, self concept and coping. *Health Education Research*, 18(4), 439–452.

Stanton, W., Lowe, J., Fisher, K., Gillespie, A. and Rose, M. (1999). Beliefs about smoking cessation among out-of-school youth. *Drug and Alcohol Dependence*, 54(3), 251–258.

Sweeting, H. and West, P. (2001). Social class and smoking at 15: The effect of different definitions of smoking. *Addiction*, 96, 1357–1359.

Tapper, A., McKinney, S., Nashmi, R., Schwarz, J., Deshpande, P., Labarca, C., Whiteaker, P., Marks, M., Collins, A. and Lester, H. (2004). Nicotine activation of $\alpha 4$ Receptors: Sufficient for reward, tolerance, and sensitisation. *Science*, 306, 1029–1032.

Tucker, L. (1984). Psychological differences between adolescent smoking intenders and non-intenders. *Journal of Psychology*, 118, 37–43.

West, P. and Sohal, T. (2006). 'Catastrophic' pathways to smoking cessation: Findings from a national survey. *British Medical Journal*, 332, 458–460.

West, P., Sweeting, H. and Ecob, R. (1999). Family and friends' influences on the uptake of regular smoking from mid-adolescence to early adulthood. *Addiction*, 94(9), 1397–1412.

Willemse, B., Postma, D., Timens, W. and ten Hacken, N. (2004). High cessation rates of cigarette smoking in subjects with and without COPD. *Chest*, 128, 3685–3687.

Wu, P., Wilson, K., Dimoulas, P. and Mills, E.J. (2006). Effectiveness of smoking cessation therapies: A systematic review and meta-analysis. *BMC Public Health*, 6, 300.

Chapter 9
Holistic issues
Carol Kelly

The progressive, degenerative and debilitating nature of COPD manifests not only in the physical cost of the disease but also in complex psychological and social consequences, together with the impact on families and carers (Guthrie *et al.*, 2001; Seamark *et al.*, 2004). As an effect, COPD is a huge burden in terms of mortality and morbidity in the UK (BTS, 2006). The impact that this disease has on society both in terms of effect on individuals and the financial burden on health services has recently been given political focus (NHS Confederation, 2004; DH, 2004; GMS, 2006). The NICE guidelines (2004a) recognised the need for palliative care to address this, calling for families and carers to have access to a full range of services, offered by multidisciplinary palliative care teams.

When considering these holistic aspects of managing COPD it becomes essential to integrate palliation of symptoms and end-of-life issues into all patient management plans.

Palliative care is similar to but distinct from terminal care. The management of severe COPD has a large palliative care element and focuses on symptom control and optimising quality of life (NICE, 2004a). Although it is clear that COPD patients have physical and psychological needs that are at least as severe as those of patients with lung cancer, provision of palliative care services are not equitable (Gore *et al.*, 2000). This in part may be due to the fact that the clinical course of the disease is unpredictable: a gradual decline in lung function that is often punctuated by exacerbations and is often heterogeneous in nature. The SUPPORT study (Lynn *et al.*, 2000) highlighted the plight of patients in the last six months of life illustrating that most patients had significant co-morbidities; 15 to 25 per cent of the patients' last six months was spent in hospital, one-quarter of patients had serious pain throughout and two-thirds had serious dyspnoea.

COPD has long been regarded as a 'self-inflicted' disease which has resulted in an undeserved therapeutic nihilism. Contributing to this is a lack of knowledge and education regarding management strategies. However, despite the degenerative nature of the disease it is now known that much can be done to restore a sense of well-being, improve quality of life, increase exercise capacity and reduce morbidity and mortality. And it is this new comprehensive holistic approach to managing patients with COPD that can truly make a difference to their outcome and alleviate the frustration of clinicians that has so often resulted in an apathetic approach to care in the past. Despite this awareness, however, the current situation regarding the provision of holistic care for patients with COPD is still severely lacking.

Psychosocial impact

Psychosocial impact

When a patient is informed that they have developed COPD they need to make a number of behavioural, social and psychological adjustments. As health professionals it is important not to ignore the patient's psychological state when treating their physical condition. Inevitably, the impact of diagnosis changes the way that people view themselves, their lives and their future and this needs to be considered in both terms of assessing and caring for COPD patients. Patients' perception of their disease can be more important than the disease itself. A succession of distressing physical, psychological and spiritual responses often challenge personal resources for coping (Williams & Bury, 1989).

Living with COPD can impact on the patient and family in a number of different ways. The individual will face many day-to-day challenges. Lifestyles inevitably have to change and this will involve adapting. The way people adjust to their disease can determine their own coping strategies and these can be dependent on many factors. For some, despite daily frustrations and challenges, they seem to adjust well and remain optimistic. Others find adjustment less easy, sometimes employing inappropriate coping strategies which can often compound their difficulties. By recognising these problems health professionals can assist patients to manage their illness more effectively. However, despite a high incidence of psychological effects of living with COPD it has been reported that less than 20 per cent of these patients had received help with this aspect of their condition (Elkington *et al.*, 2005). This neglect can impact further on the patient by causing loss of dignity and putting additional pressures on carers and families.

Feeling positive or negative about oneself influences the quality of everyday experiences. Patients with COPD are often confronted with issues that may affect their self esteem:

- changing body image
- embarrassment (from dyspnoea, cough and sputum production)
- social position within the family (where they were the main breadwinner)
- inability to work
- financial implications
- poor mobility
- social isolation
- loss of sexual identity
- loss of independence.

(Guthrie *et al.*, 2001)

These impaired physical, emotional and social dimensions of daily living often result in a sedentary lifestyle with progressive dyspnoea and fatigue and hence the downward spiral of the disease. A feeling of control or sense of mastery over the disease is an important aspect of quality of life in coping with chronic symptoms and an individual's perception of health.

Many COPD patients also experience a sense of guilt. This can be caused by several factors including smoking and the impact that their disorder has had on their family life (Robinson, 2005). This guilt regarding the impact upon carers and relatives is so important that some patients see their quality of life as dependent on family relationships (Guthrie *et al.*, 2001). This is a phenomenon that is supported by evidence that demonstrates a positive effect from family and social networks on quality of life and health outcomes in COPD (Wong & Bourbeau, 2005).

Despite this, social isolation is common in COPD patients with severe disease (Gore *et al.*, 2000; Skilbeck *et al.*, 1998) and as COPD affects mobility, social isolation is an important consideration. Approximately half of patients leave their house less than once per month or never in the last year of their life (Elkington *et al.*, 2005). Patients often describe their loneliness and their frustration due to planned breaks such as Christmas with families being curtailed due to illness (Guthrie *et al.*, 2001). Interviews with carers of patients with COPD concluded that patients who are housebound with high levels of morbidity require community health services (Elkington *et al.*, 2004). Unfortunately such care is often lacking and often services are provided too late to be of benefit (Rhodes, 1999).

Access to social services has notoriously been difficult for respiratory patients, often because of reluctance on their part to accept the term disabled. One study reported 70 per cent of individuals and families received no support from social services in the last year of life (Elkington *et al.*, 2005), whilst Gore *et al.* (2000) clearly portrayed a situation where patients seldom receive holistic care appropriate to their needs. Lack of communication generally between health and social services does not help this situation when planning discharge or managing patients in the community.

Impact on families and carers

Impact on others

COPD has a big impact on informal carers and families (Seamark *et al.*, 2004). Carers can experience the same losses as patients and the strain on carers is clear. Rhodes (1999), through an interview-based study of the relatives of deceased COPD patients, identified that carers themselves were usually elderly and had their own health problems. Many had to give up work to care for the patient and, over the years, their caring role had become increasingly demanding and the number of tasks associated with personal care increased. This thematic narrative of experiences by relatives does provide a useful insight into the burden of carers in the last phase of life and would support the experiences of most healthcare professionals involved in caring for patients and their families. The needs of relatives and family often appear to be largely unrecognised or ignored, with little or no practical help or relief from 24-hour care. This possibly contributes to frequent hospital admissions.

After death support is often found to be lacking. One son in interview reported how his bereaved mother coped following the death of her husband: 'Caring takes over their whole life and then the person dies and you are left with nothing' (Rhodes, 1999). After death, carers often value the opportunity to discuss the illness and death (Elkington *et al.*, 2005) and perhaps this supports the notion of bereavement visits, especially by staff who have built up relationships with patients and carers, sometimes over many years.

Symptom management

Symptom management

The impact of lung cancer and COPD has been compared by interviewing carers or patients, or by directly measuring quality of life (Edmonds *et al.*, 2001; Gore *et al.*, 2000). COPD patients are more likely to experience symptoms for longer and have significantly worse limitations of activities of daily living and physical, social and emotional functioning (Gore *et al.*, 2000). In another study of COPD deaths in London (Elkington *et al.*, 2005) a remarkably high level of symptoms was reported in the 12 months before death, with 98 per cent of patients reporting breathlessness, 77 per cent low mood and poor sleep quality and 53 per cent subject to panic attacks. Unfortunately treatments offered at reducing breathlessness were only effective in 57 per cent of cases.

Despite this emerging knowledge, health professionals seem to lack confidence in caring for patients with non-malignant disease. This may be due to the unpredictable nature of the disease trajectory, often prolonged with the dying phase not always easily recognisable. This insidious deterioration is often interspersed with acute exacerbations further compounding the unpredictability of the prognosis.

Patients' experience of symptoms cannot be predicted by calculating disease severity, as COPD effects people in different ways. Indeed patients deal with symptoms differently, and the effect of these symptoms on quality of life is variable. Predominant symptoms are dyspnoea and depression but other symptoms such as coughing, fatigue, pain, anorexia and thirst are also commonly described (Lynn *et al.*, 2000; Edmonds *et al.*, 2001; Elkington *et al.*, 2004). The additional result of these symptoms is often reduced exercise tolerance and recurrent hospital admissions. Loss of dignity, social isolation and psychosocial problems are further exacerbated at this stage.

Alleviation of symptoms can therefore be seen as a priority in holistic management. For pharmacological relief of major symptoms, airflow obstruction and hypoxaemia should be optimally treated according to evidence-based guidelines (NICE, 2004a), as discussed in other chapters. For the purpose of this chapter, non-pharmacological and some specific pharmacological approaches aimed at palliation of symptoms will be considered.

Dyspnoea

Dyspnoea

The main disabling manifestation of the disease is dyspnoea, which is often disabling despite maximum treatment. Dyspnoea is a perception of breathlessness and therefore needs to be considered as a subjective view of the patient. It correlates poorly with lung function (Celli *et al.*, 2004) and is certainly one of the most overwhelming and distressing symptoms experienced by patients in end-stage disease. Perception is affected by more than physiological variables and successful alleviation of perceived symptoms can cause dramatic improvements in both physical and psychological comfort.

Dyspnoea is interrelated with anxiety (Brenes, 2003) and as such can manifest in a vicious cycle of fear and produce a self-perpetuating negative feedback mechanism. In addition, the patient may be experiencing emotional reactions, such as anger, guilt, denial and fear (Madge & Esmond, 2001). Added to any depression, anxiety and panic, the cycle of breathlessness becomes relentless and will continue to worsen unless management strategies are incorporated.

Figure 9.1

The vicious cycle of breathlessness

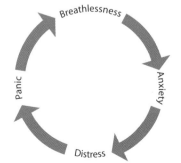

Management of dyspnoea is individual and sometimes a 'trial and error' approach is necessary, often combining several strategies. Approaches to management of dyspnoea include positioning, breathing control, oxygen therapy, opioids and psychological interventions. As Krishnasamy *et al.* (2001) indicate, effective therapy can only be achieved once the nature and impact of breathlessness have been understood from the perspective of the individual experiencing it. It is therefore important to treat breathlessness holistically rather than simply offering bronchodilator therapy.

Positioning and breathing control

Teaching and establishing effective breathing patterns and airway clearance techniques can reduce the experience of dyspnoea, the overall aim being to reduce the work of breathing and increase confidence. This is achieved through maximisation of the respiratory muscles and enhancing diaphragmatic displacement.

Positioning can help tremendously in affecting dyspnoea. Again this is individual and patients' adoption of comfortable positions can vary with some patients adopting one position for long periods, while others prefer to vary position frequently. Some patients will prefer to sit rather than lie and certainly a common occurrence on respiratory wards is for patients to die in armchairs rather than in bed. The use of pillows can be beneficial and this can be further enhanced with bed tables or forward positioning enabling the patient to adopt the orthopnoeic position.

Figure 9.2

The orthopnoeic position

Teaching and reinforcing breathing control techniques is considered an essential approach for managing dyspnoea. In particular, therapists will commonly use the active cycle of breathing with forced expirations to enhance expectoration and clear secretions. However, to date there is little empirical evidence of a sound methodological nature to support these strategies in COPD.

Conversely, studies have demonstrated that techniques and strategies for breathing control in lung cancer patients considerably improve the patients' ability to self-care and reduce their levels of dyspnoea and distress (Corner *et al.*, 1996; Bredin *et al.*, 1999). This approach has recently been developed into breathlessness clinics for patients with lung cancer, demonstrating a reduction in patients experiencing breathlessness several times per day from 73 per cent to 27 per cent (Hately *et al.*, 2003). It is difficult to extrapolate this evidence from one lung pathology to another. However it may be a model upon which existing evidence involving COPD patients can be incorporated into organisation and delivery of care.

Oxygen

Oxygen should be used to correct hypoxaemia but it is also commonly prescribed to reduce breathlessness. There is, however, little evidence that short-burst oxygen use is of benefit in COPD as Booth *et al.* (2004) concluded in their comprehensive literature review. Unfortunately, patients and carers often perceive oxygen therapy as lifesaving, a view also held by many well-meaning but misinformed healthcare professionals. Slightly more positive findings were observed in one randomised, single blind placebo study by Stevenson and Calverley (2004). The authors demonstrated that oxygen used on recovery from exercise reduced the duration of dynamic hyperinflation, but this did not decrease dyspnoea or alter the speed of recovery. It is hypothesised that this reduction in dynamic hyperinflation could account for the relief gained by short-burst oxygen but this was only in relation to exercise and would only apply to a carefully selected group.

Caution with any palliative approach should always be aired in order to prevent the introduction of new symptoms. For example, exacerbation of hypercapnia caused by injudicious use of oxygen could induce drowsiness or headaches. There is no physiological rationale for administering oxygen to patients with an SaO_2 of more than 92 per cent at rest and patients who experience relief are probably experiencing a placebo effect from facial cooling and relief of anxiety (Muers, 2005). Fan therapy or an open window can often have similar benefits to the use of oxygen through the cooling effects stimulating the facial nerves (Schwartzstein, 1987); nebulisers probably work in a similar way.

Other drawbacks of using oxygen as a placebo are that it may cause psychological dependence and may interfere with the relationships between carers and patients. However, despite these considerations, oxygen continues to be recommended for use in the palliation of dyspnoea in patients who are normoxaemic and not relieved by other treatments (NICE, 2004a; www.bnf.org, accessed on 1.8.07). Although assessment of blood gases is not normally required in this situation, attention to pulse oximetry, aiming to keep oxygen saturation around 92 per cent, will usually avoid exacerbation of hypercapnia (Murphy *et al.*, 2001). Booth *et al.* (2004) support the notion of assessment advising that a formal assessment, perhaps with symptom diaries, should be made regarding the efficacy of oxygen in respect of reduction in dyspnoea and improvement in quality of life. NICE guidelines (2004a) also suggest that this therapy should only be continued if an improvement in breathlessness following therapy has been documented. For patients receiving LTOT (long-term oxygen therapy) other issues and problems exist that further impact on psychosocial wellbeing and need addressing by healthcare professionals (Ring & Danielson, 1997).

Oxygen therapy remains a controversial issue in palliative care. In view of the juxtaposed and incongruous clinical positions of short-burst oxygen therapy and the spiralling costs of oxygen this is clearly an area that needs urgent investment in further research.

Opioids

The use of opioids in managing breathlessness has recently been addressed through a meta-analysis (Jennings *et al.*, 2003). Eighteen studies were analysed, nine of which concerned nebulised opioids; no overall beneficial effects were found on exercise tolerance or dyspnoea with nebulised opioids but a small effect was measured on reduction in breathlessness with non-nebulised preparations. It has been hypothesised that opioids reduce dyspnoea by action comparable to pain relief (Muers, 2002), modulating perception of dyspnoea without necessarily altering either the ventilatory drive or the ventilation response itself. In larger doses, however, there will still probably be a reduction in ventilatory drive, together with a reduction in conscious level. Side effects therefore need to be considered especially in larger doses.

Muers (2002) suggests management of dyspnoea in three stages: mild, moderate and severe. Mild and moderate dyspnoea should still focus on treating the cause; in the case of COPD this would include bronchodilators, breathing control, exercise and management of anxiety. Once the dyspnoea becomes more profound opioids need to be considered in smaller doses, with withdrawal if no benefit. Dosage of morphine in the meta-analysis (Jennings *et al.*, 2003) varied and included parenteral as well as oral administration and some cancer patients. As a guidance however, Cheshire and Merseyside Integrated Cancer Network (2006) suggest oral morphine sulphate solution commencing at an initial low dose of 2.5 mg four times per day and as needed three to four hourly; this can be titrated upwards every 48 hours as needed and tolerated, for the treatment of dyspnoea in end-stage chronic respiratory disease. This needs to be concurrent with other strategies such as oxygen, exercise and anxiety management, amongst others.

Psychological care

Psychological interventions for management of dyspnoea can include techniques such as distraction therapy, relaxation techniques and some forms of complementary therapies (see below). Alleviation of fears can be addressed through involving the patient family in decision-making, for example about the use of opioids or NIV, enabling the patient to feel more informed and in control. Any strategies that can enhance coping abilities and relieve symptoms will ultimately be of benefit.

Anxiety and depression

Studies that involve interviewing patients (Guthrie *et al.*, 2001; Robinson, 2005; Seamark *et al.*, 2004) identify other ways that patients can be affected by their disorder. Panic and anxiety are common, as are loss of personal liberty and dignity. It is important to remember that panic and anxiety also contribute to breathlessness and COPD patients clearly have physical triggers for anxiety (Elkington *et al.*, 2004). Dyspnoea, although a physiological response, is a subjective view of the patient and has been closely associated with anxiety (Brenes, 2003).

Patients with COPD are also regularly found to be depressed (Elkington *et al.*, 2005). When lung cancer and COPD patients were compared, anxiety and depression scores suggested that 90 per cent of patients with COPD suffered clinically relevant anxiety or depression compared to 52 per cent of patients with lung cancer (Gore *et al.*, 2000). In addition, symptoms such as breathlessness and depression are at best only partly relieved. In one study (Elkington *et al.*, 2005), 82 per cent of sufferers received no interventions for depression or low mood.

The incidence of depression in patients with COPD has long since been recognised (Dow & Mest, 1997). However, in many patients psychological problems are often left unrecognised and therefore untreated. This is partly because it is difficult to distinguish between the physical symptoms of respiratory dysfunction and psychological conditions.

Pharmacological approaches are valuable in treating depression, panic attacks and insomnia. However cognitive behavioural therapies (Heslop & Rao, 2003) and exploration of patient fears are also important. Discussion, reassurance and practical support for patients and carers can contribute enormously to the alleviation of psychological and emotional responses.

Fatigue

Fatigue, a very common symptom of severe COPD, is a subjective experience that can have a profound effect on quality of life (Barnett, 2006). It can be described as an overwhelming desire to rest and sleep and, although little empirical evidence exists that relates fatigue to COPD, some authors have attempted to clarify it (Trendall, 2000; Small & Lamb, 1999). Fatigue will impact on the ability to carry out daily activities and patients often cope with it through the development of various strategies such as conservation of energy and planning ahead. Concept analysis has shown fatigue is distinctly different from depression and dyspnoea (Trendall, 2000); however it remains poorly defined in the literature.

Management of other symptoms

Although dyspnoea is the main presenting symptom in COPD, other physical symptoms can manifest and, if not dealt with, can further compound existing anxiety and discomfort which, in turn, will aggravate dyspnoea. Table 9.1 shows common symptoms and examples of some interventions that may be useful. It is not exhaustive and you should refer to more detailed guidelines (www.bnf.org; NICE, 2004a & 2004b) for a more comprehensive account.

Table 9.1

Pharmacological and non-pharmacological management

Symptom	Pharmacological Management	Non-pharmacological Management
Dyspnoea	Bronchodilators Opioids Oxygen	Fan Position Breathing control Anxiety management Occupational therapy lifestyle adjustments Complementary therapies
Viscous secretions	Nebulised saline	Adequate hydration Humidification Physiotherapy assistance
Anxiety	Benzodiazepines Opioids	Oxygen (placebo) Complementary therapies
Cough	Cough Cough suppressants Mucolytics Nebulised saline Reverse cause e.g. excessive secretions	Positioning Acupuncture Physiotherapy
Dry mouth	Artificial saliva preparations Consider cause and treat, e.g. thrush	Ice cubes Hydration Humidification

Fatigue	Treat contributing factors,
	  e.g. depression
	Query side effects of any
	  medication
		Energy conservation
		Breathing control
		Nutritional support

Depression	Antidepressants Night sedation Anxiolytics Consider nicotine withdrawal and treat	Counselling Cognitive behavioural therapy Treat any underlying issues

Communication

Communication is central to holistic care for patients with any chronic disease. Health professionals need to be aware of the way information is communicated to patients and to be able to understand patients' feelings. Appropriate communication skills are critical in ensuring that interventions are beneficial and that a trusting relationship is established between the healthcare professional and their patient. Sullivan *et al.* (1996) identified themes regarding communication with end-stage COPD patients, highlighting common difficulties experienced by physicians initiating discussion about ventilation. These included not knowing when to do it, what to say, their own feelings of awkwardness and not really 'knowing' the patient. They said that knowing a patient helped them determine whether they were ready for the discussion and increased their sensitivity to a patient's responses during the discussion. The skill is to have the ability to provide information in a sensitive and supportive way and to offer time, especially when addressing prognosis. This allows the patient and family the opportunity to explore issues together at their own pace (Madge & Esmond, 2001). Unfortunately, the clinical reality is that time is limited.

In the development of communication with patients, it is essential to listen to and learn from patients about their needs and how these should be met. One of the biggest challenges when trying to improve care for COPD patients will be finding ways of talking about end of life without necessarily making them feel that they are preparing for imminent death.

Education

Educating patients regarding their disease and how to live within their limits should be expected to increase confidence and enable better self-management, however research evidence is sparse. Education can be incorporated into pulmonary rehabilitation programmes or carried out as part of routine consultation. Examples of topics that may be included are:

- information about the disease itself
- treatment options
- advice on nutrition
- smoking cessation
- anxiety management

- financial benefits
- consequences for relationships and sexuality
- the benefits of physical exercise
- relaxation
- self-management
- travel
- energy conservation and pacing
- support groups.

This approach could lead to an improvement in a patient's well-being, resulting in increased self-esteem and quality of life. Self-management will enable patients to recognise and respond early to signs of an exacerbation. A systematic review of the evidence regarding self-management plans suggested that their use resulted in greater use of short courses of oral corticosteroids and antibiotics (Monninkhof *et al.*, 2003). This in turn could impact on the disease trajectory through early intervention and possibly even prevention of exacerbations. However, the overall conclusion of the review was that there was currently insufficient data to make recommendations and there existed no definitive evidence that self-management worked in COPD outside an exercise programme. Clearly, further research is required.

In the palliative care context the use of education may also contribute positively to a 'supportive care' approach (Ahmedzai & Walsh, 2000). This approach is not restricted to the end of life but is determined by physical, psychological, information, rehabilitation and existential needs – from the time of diagnosis and regardless of prognosis. Supportive care embraces palliative care for the terminal stages but if offered from the onset of a chronic illness it should result in a seamless, holistic package of care.

Complementary therapies

There has been a great deal of interest in the use of complementary therapies. The House of Lords Select Committee for Science and Technology's report (2000) suggested randomised-controlled trials are the best means of researching the area. Some patients look for alternatives to orthodox medicine for several reasons including the avoidance of side effects associated with drugs and the perception that those alternatives are 'natural' and therefore safe. In these situations it is the responsibility of the healthcare professional to acknowledge these interventions and guide the patient in their choice, considering efficacy and safety and encouraging the use of these therapies as complementary to, rather than alternative to, conventional medicine.

Ernst *et al.* (1995) define complementary medicine as 'diagnosis, treatment and/or prevention' which complements mainstream medicine by contributing to a common whole. One of the major drawbacks to such treatments is that evidence of effectiveness is often sparse and some may have adverse effects; there is also a possibility of exploitation of vulnerable patients. Although evidence is accumulating in the use of complementary therapies to manage asthma there remains a scarcity in COPD care.

Filshie & White (2005) in their appraisal of complementary therapies discussed evidence that the use of acupuncture for the treatment of dyspnoea showed a significant benefit over the control group for both dyspnoea and exercise tolerance. In addition a later study by Maa *et al.* (1997) demonstrated that acupressure reduced dyspnoea, as measured on a visual analogue scale, compared to sham acupressure. Yogic breathing exercises were also identified as superior to physiotherapy breathing exercises for exercise tolerance, recovery and control of acute attacks of shortness of breath (Filshie & White, 2005). A recent appraisal of the effectiveness of herbal medicines in treating COPD was conducted through a systematic review of the evidence (Guo *et al.*, 2006). Due to the heterogeneity of the data, statistical pooling was not performed. The authors concluded that, currently, the evidence from randomised clinical trials is scarce and often methodologically weak and called for more rigorously-designed studies.

A preliminary report on a randomised-controlled trial examining the effects of reflexology treatments on COPD demonstrated some positive effects. Results were qualitative and quantitative and showed that there are a number of areas of possible benefit for patients with COPD, but a larger study with a longer timeframe is needed for a full evaluation (Wilkinson *et al.*, 2006).

The consensus seems to be that evidence is still scarce regarding the use of any complementary therapies for COPD patients. The British Lung Foundation has a fact sheet on complementary therapies for patients, however the information is limited (www.britishlungfoundation.org).

Nutrition

Low body weight is common in people with COPD, especially as their disease progresses and nutritional depletion with cachexia and muscle wasting are now becoming recognised as features of severe COPD (Schols & Wouters, 2000). Although linked to increasing evidence that COPD is a disease with systemic inflammatory effects (Agusti, 2005), the causes of this weight loss are multifactorial, including increased energy expenditure, poor calorie intake and flattening of the diaphragm due to hyperinflation. Poor calorie intake can be a result of multiple factors including:

- depression and fatigue
- dyspnoea (affecting shopping, food preparation and chewing)
- reduced appetite
- reduced finances
- oxygen/inhaled medication side effects.

In addition, cachexia, a metabolic inability to use nutrients effectively, results not only in weight loss but also loss of muscle, anorexia, chronic nausea and weakness leading to malnutrition and debility. This further exacerbates decreased respiratory muscle strength and increases dyspnoea; it can impair heart and lung function and reduce the ability to exercise and recover. The systemic effects of inflammatory cytokines, particularly TNF-α, can also lead to muscle apoptosis. In COPD this is further compounded by a decreased food intake as a result of breathlessness, altered absorption as a result of hypoxia and increased resting energy expenditure as a result of the increased work of breathing (Schols & Wouters, 2000).

For all these reasons, nutrition is becoming an increasingly important consideration in holistic management of COPD. Low body mass index (BMI) is associated with higher mortality (Landbo *et al.*, 1999) and it is reversible (Schols *et al.*, 1998). Therefore assessment and treatment of nutritional depletion are important management strategies. Calculation of BMI should be considered essential in both initial and ongoing assessment of COPD patients (see figure 9.3).

However, despite NICE guidance (2004) to provide nutritional supplements to COPD patients with a low BMI a systematic review, Ferreira *et al.* (2005), concluded that there is no evidence to support simple nutritional supplementation in these patients. This review of 12 studies included 392 patients and concluded that nutritional support had no significant effect on anthropometric measures, lung function or exercise capacity in patients with stable COPD. More research is needed. There is a growing body of evidence however that suggests exercise augments nutritional supplementation by increasing muscle mass (Griffiths & Proud, 2005; Fuld *et al.*, 2005) and there is clearly a need for further research in this area. One thing certainly worth considering if using nutritional supplements is that they should not be used as substitutes to replace normal dietary intake.

Sometimes simple advice regarding eating little and often and fortifying food to increase calories without bulk (for example, grating cheese into mashed potatoes; adding powdered milk to full fat milk) is the most appropriate from both a clinical and practical point of view.

Figure 9.3

Body mass index

Calculating BMI

$$BMI = \frac{weight \ (kg)}{height^2 \ (m)}$$

BMI and nutritional status

< 18.5 – underweight

18.5–24.9 – normal

25–29.5 – overweight

> 30 – obese

Non-invasive ventilation (NIV) in palliative care

The use of NIV in acute exacerbation of COPD is now well established. Some of this early work also demonstrated an effect of NIV on dyspnoea (Bott *et al.*, 1993), suggesting a benefit in end-stage care, although evidence is limited. NIV in these circumstances is aimed at ameliorating symptoms related to hypercapnia, for example headaches and poor sleep quality, and can potentially buy time. Under these circumstances the goal of NIV should always be decided in advance and the burden of NIV needs to be outweighed against any advantages. Case studies carried out by Shee and Green (2003) demonstrated some effects (five out of ten case studies were COPD patients) and predicted an increase in the use of domiciliary NIV for COPD patients, while cautioning that these patients should be carefully selected.

End-of-life care

Psychosocial consequences and physiological symptoms clearly are a great burden to patients, in addition to depression, but fear of death is also common (Guthrie *et al.*, 2001; Elkington *et al.*, 2005). Researchers comment that these feelings are often voiced in the strongest language (Guthrie *et al.*, 2001) such as 'what a way to go!' and 'I'm terrified'. Often death from respiratory failure has been witnessed during admissions to hospital resulting in a fear of the experience of dying as distinct from a fear of death (Clark, 2003). Given this near and repeatedly threatening approach of death, an extension of a palliative approach to end-stage COPD is clearly merited.

However, due to the unpredictable trajectory of the disease, planning for death can present complex challenges; a form of palliative care needs to be developed without the connotations of palliative and hospice care. Deciding when to change the approach from aggressive to palliative management is often convoluted in COPD, with both strategies often co-existing. Decisions should be collaborative between the patient, carers and healthcare professionals to enable participation in an informed and active manner.

Several major barriers have been identified to planning end-of-life care in COPD patients (Sullivan *et al.*, 1996); prognosis is difficult and, possibly as a consequence, may be deferred and patients may not realise that they have reached a terminal phase in their condition. Current initiatives aim to improve end-of-life care by ensuring more patients die in the place of their choice, usually at home (DH, 2003). In Elkington *et al.*, (2005) study significantly more carers of patients who died at home felt this was the right place to die, as opposed to informants of those who died in hospital ($p = 0.008$).

Palliative care provision

Palliative care is defined by the World Health Organisation (Sepúlveda *et al.*, 2002) as a holistic approach to caring for patients with life-threatening disease and their families, which integrates physical, psychosocial and spiritual aspects of care, whatever the stage of their illness. The key principles underpinning palliative care have been highlighted as:

- a focus on quality of life, which includes good symptom control
- a whole-person approach, taking into account the patient's past life experience and current situation
- care which encompasses both the person, the families and the carers
- respect for autonomy and choice
- open and sensitive communication (extending to carers and healthcare professionals).

(Tebbit, 1999)

The National Council for Hospice and Specialist Palliative Care (NCHSPC) declared in 2001 that all patients with palliative care needs, together with their carers, should have equitable access to a range of specialist palliative care services appropriate to their needs. Despite their embracing of non-malignant terminal diseases in this way, provision of services has been slow to respond. As a result there is currently a lack of resources for COPD palliative care in some areas, or a reluctance to allocate resources. According to a retrospective survey of the informants of 399 deaths from COPD in London (Elkington *et al.*, 2005), patients who died from COPD lacked surveillance and received inadequate services from primary and secondary care in the year before they died. Other studies (Gore *et al.*, 2000) show that, although lung cancer patients could receive help from specialist palliative care services, patients with COPD could not.

Communication with patients about their prognosis and end-of-life care is also lacking. Modern palliative care advocates open communication between health professionals and patients and this includes providing information about prognosis. Most patients know that they are going to die (Guthrie *et al.*, 2001; Edmonds *et al.*, 2001) and when interviewed they state that they need better communication about their diagnosis and prognosis (Robinson, 2005). But few report discussing the matter with their physician (Knauft *et al.*, 2005). Some studies report that as few as eight per cent of patients are given the opportunity to discuss their prognosis with their doctor (Edmonds *et al.*, 2001). Perhaps this is because health professionals underestimate the emotional impact of the disease and prognosis?

Management of COPD in primary and secondary care

Elkington *et al.* (2001) asked 214 London GPs about this subject, and, while 75 per cent thought discussions of prognosis were often necessary or essential in severe COPD, and the majority (82 per cent) felt that GPs have an important role in this respect, only 41 per cent had discussed prognosis. Amongst those who reported rarely or never discussing prognosis, a majority felt ill-prepared to discuss the subject, some finding it hard to start discussions with patients. The authors conclude that the palliative care approach to open communication is not applied routinely, and that uncertainty among GPs about how patients view the discussion of prognosis, alongside inadequate preparation, may pose potential barriers. The consequences are that often patients may not realise that their condition has reached a terminal phase and planning is problematic.

A British Lung Foundation Survey (BLF, 2006) found that 34 per cent of patients do not understand that their condition will get worse and over half of respondents said their GP did not discuss emotional aspects of COPD with them. This supported a report recently released by the Healthcare Commission (2006), entitled 'Clearing the Air'. This report highlights the poor provision of palliative care services for those with COPD. It identifies a need for improved access to services and recommends that Primary Care Trusts should monitor access to, and provision of, palliative care for people with non-cancer diagnoses.

Advance directives

Heffner *et al.* (1997) carried out a prospective evaluation of advance directive education during a pulmonary rehabilitation programme. The researchers found that the group that received instruction were considerably more likely to discuss issues and preferences related to death, again emphasising the importance of open communication. Knauft *et al.* (2005) utilising a focus group analysis of oxygen-dependent COPD patients and their physicians found that only 32 per cent of patients had discussed end-of-life care with their physicians.

Clinicians often find difficulty initiating such discussions. Barriers identified by the physicians included too little time in appointments and not wanting to take away patients' hope; patient barriers included lack of continuity of physicians and concentrating on staying alive. Both groups found it easier not to talk about it.

Facilitators of communication included patients' experiences of friends or family dying and patients feeling that physicians saw them as people rather than cases. There also appears to be a degree of conflict between making decisions and acting on them. Golin *et al.* (2000) looked prospectively at resuscitation preferences. Of patients who had completed advanced directives, 63 per cent had not told their physician what they were.

How a proactive approach to palliative care is adopted will be individual to both patients and healthcare professionals, building upon previous experiences and often with conflicting narratives between an acceptance of inevitable death and an optimistic view of hope. Sullivan *et al.* (1996) suggest that these discussions should take place when the patient is stable and that there is a need to 'know' the patient in order to understand their perception of their quality of life, their satisfaction with current functioning and their expectation of life. Attitudes to resuscitation cannot be predicted from disease severity or age. Although prognosis is an inexact science, prognostic uncertainty should not lead clinicians to fall into prognostic paralysis (Gaber *et al.*, 2004; Murray *et al.*, 2005). They should ask themselves 'Would I be surprised if my patient were to die in the next 12 months?' If the answer to this question is 'No', planning for a good death should be the adopted strategy, rather than just monitoring a downward set of physical variables. Although circumstances for each patient should be considered individually this could be a useful pragmatic clinical benchmark.

Place of death

The place of final care for patients with any terminal illness tends to be influenced more by resource availability rather than patient choice. This seems particularly evident for individuals with COPD. Improvements in organisation and delivery of care are needed. This in turn should result in:

- greater choice for patients in where they wish to live and die

- decrease in the number of emergency admissions

- decrease in the number of people transferred from a care home during the last week of life.

Models of care

In the UK, opportunities exist to initiate an approach whereby patients who 'reasonably might die' could be identified and palliative care management initiated. The general practitioner contract (GMS, 2006) has resulted in the establishment of comprehensive registers for COPD. Although the contracts have been much criticised, practices have been incentivised for doing regular assessments and investigations that would facilitate the identification of patients entering the final phase of life. This should enable healthcare professionals to ensure optimisation of symptom management and address any psychosocial issues that may be apparent.

Currently there are no national palliative care guidelines for this group of patients who have unmet physical, psychological and spiritual needs but there are some examples of good practice. The Cheshire and Merseyside Integrated Cancer Network (2006) is one example where a working party was set up to look at the needs of all patients with end-stage chronic lung disease. The resulting guidelines (www.arms.co.uk) have empowered generalists and raised awareness of issues regarding symptom management and referral.

The Liverpool Care Pathway for the dying patient (LCP) (Liverpool Care of the Dying Pathway, www.lcp-mariecurie.org.uk) has been developed to transfer the hospice model of care into other care settings. A multi-professional document proving an evidence-based framework for end-of-life care, the LCP has been successfully implemented for patients dying with both malignant and non-malignant disease. It incorporates not only physical comfort but also psychological and spiritual care, as well as family support. It is a key recommendation in the NICE guidelines for supportive and palliative care in cancer (NICE, 2004b) and is an NHS Beacon project (www.modernnhs.nhs.uk/nhsbeacons).

Assessment of holistic impact of disease

Holistic impact

The evaluation of medical treatment has traditionally been based on clinical, laboratory and radiological tests. However, with growing interest in patient-centred outcomes, a variety of validated tools have become available. These are often generic measures of health status but some disease-specific tools are available and have been well evaluated (Singh *et al.*, 2001). In particular, The St. George's Respiratory Questionnaire (Jones *et al.*, 1992) is a popular one used to assess respiratory patients. A good quality of life tool should contain measurable objective components such as income, housing, physical functioning, work, socio-economic status and support networks, in addition to subjective components such as attitudes, perceptions, aspirations, and frustrations.

There are also a number of validated psychological assessment scales, such as the Acceptance of Illness Scale (Weinman *et al.*, 1984) and the Hospital Anxiety and Depression Scale (Snaith & Zigmond, 1994). These scales do risk requiring patients to focus on issues such as dependency on others and feelings of hopelessness and inadequacy, however, and so caution needs to be exercised. Any issues raised will need to be addressed. Dyspnoea is commonly assessed using the MRC dyspnoea scale (see Chapter 4). This is a simple, well-validated, patient-friendly tool that requires little time for completion.

Mortality as such used to be predicted using lung function alone. However, due to the complex pathophysiology involved in assessing COPD holistically, the use of a multidimensional staging tool has now been advocated (Celli *et al.*, 2004). This involves assessment not only of lung function but also BMI, dyspnoea and exercise capacity.

Research and ethical considerations

One reason for the paucity of research concerning proposed interventions in palliation of COPD is the difficulty of recruiting subjects into research projects, which presents ethical dilemmas; in addition attrition rates from these studies (certainly those looking at severe end-stage disease) are high, even in the early stages of the study (Cook *et al.*, 2002; Grande & Todd, 2000). This is not only due to patients and families not wishing to take part in research. Ewing *et al.* (2004) also identified gate-keeping hurdles from ethics committees. Hopkinson *et al.* (2005) propose a participatory approach to enable successful recruitment that challenges the belief that it is inappropriate to study people at the end of life by allowing clinical practice and research to share decision-making.

Ethical issues that may be encountered in administering care for patients with end-stage COPD include respect for autonomy. Consulting individuals and obtaining informed consent should ensure that autonomy is respected. The issue of beneficence (doing good) versus non-maleficence (doing no harm) is often met when trying to palliate symptoms without causing further discomfort or introducing new symptoms. Consideration of NIV and oxygen therapy, for example, can often produce dilemmas that need to be addressed. Again, careful consultation with patients and family in decision-making processes can help to ensure autonomy is respected. Finally, the issue of justice may be breached in the inequitable distribution and therefore access to resources. This is particularly evident in the provision of NIV services (both acute and domiciliary) and availability of hospice care.

Summary

It is clear that many COPD patients have substantial symptom burden and unmet palliative care needs and that health professionals can feel ill-equipped to interact in a therapeutic manner. Even when patients are referred there is little research on which to base interventions and palliative care education for clinicians tends to focus primarily on malignant disorders.

These unmet needs may be a source of frustration to well-meaning healthcare professionals but there are, however, many things that can be done. Even with no cure there is much that can be achieved to improve patients' quality of life and health professionals can work together to help patients manage their illness more effectively. Acknowledging that COPD has an emotional impact is important, as is inviting patients to discuss this impact and using active listening strategies to encourage the patient to express their feelings. It is also possible to assess for clinically significant anxiety or depression and to refer if appropriate. Support groups such as the British Lung Foundation's 'Breathe Easy' are beneficial to some and the British Lung Foundation can also offer the support of specialist nurses in some areas.

Respiratory disease may be one of the greatest challenges for healthcare provision in the future. The NICE guidelines on the management of COPD (NICE, 2004a) clearly indicate that patients with end-stage COPD and their families and carers should have access to a full range of palliative care services, and the forthcoming national service framework is likely to highlight this neglected aspect of COPD care as a priority for service design and provision. In order to implement such strategies, we need to add to our knowledge base in this area through research and to enhance the provision of services through participation in discussion groups, panels, and guideline committees.

Importantly, from a clinical perspective, recognition of the disease trajectory in the last few years of life, together with early intervention with education, psychosocial support and symptom palliation, can alter the holistic care of these patients. It needs a concerted focus on the healthcare agenda and better education of healthcare professionals in the issues.

References

Agusti, A.G. (2005). COPD – a multicomponent disease: Implications for management. *Respiratory Medicine*, 99(6), 670–682.

Ahmedzai, S.H. and Walsh, T.D. (2000). Palliative medicine and modern cancer care. *Seminars in Oncology*, 27, 1–6.

Barnett, M. (2006). Providing palliative care in end-stage COPD within primary care. *Journal of Community Nursing*, 20(3), 30–34.

Booth, S., Anderson, H., Swannick, M., Wade, R., Kite, S. and Johnson, M. (2004). The use of oxygen in the palliation of breathlessness. A report of the Expert Working Group of the Scientific Committee of the Association of Palliative Medicine. *Respiratory Medicine*, 98, 66–77.

Bott, J., Carroll, M.P. and Conway, J.H. (1993). Randomised controlled trial of nasal ventilation in acute ventilatory failure due to COPD. *Lancet*, 341, 1555–1557.

Bredin, M., Corner, J., Krishnasamy, M., Plant, H., Bailey, C. and A'Hern, R. (1999). Multi-centre randomised controlled trial of nursing intervention for breathlessness in patients with lung cancer. *British Medical Journal*, 318, 888–889.

Brenes, G.A. (2003). Anxiety and COPD: Prevalence, impact and treatment. *Psychosomatic Medicine*, 65, 963–970.

British Lung Foundation (2006). *Lost in Translation: Bridging the Communication Gap in COPD*. London: BLF.

British Thoracic Society (BTS) (2006). *The Burden of Lung Disease*, 2nd edn. London: BTS.

Celli, B.R., Cote, C.G., Marin, J.M., Casanova, C., Montes de Oca, M., Mendez, R.A., Pinto Plata, V. and Cabral, H.J. (2004). The body-mass index, airflow obstruction, dyspnoea and exercise capacity index in chronic obstructive pulmonary disease. *New England Journal of Medicine*, 350(10), 1005–1012.

Cheshire and Merseyside Integrated Cancer Network (2006). Specialist palliative care referral guidelines and symptom control for patients with end-stage chronic respiratory disease. Available at www.arns.co.uk/Guidelines.html, accessed 1.8.07.

Clark, J. (2003). Patient-centred death. *British Medical Journal*, 237, 174–175.

Cook, A.M., Finlay, I.G. and Butler-Keating, R.J. (2002). Recruiting into palliative care trials: Lessons learnt from a feasibility study. *Palliative Medicine*, 16, 163–165.

Corner, J., Plant, H., A'Hern, R. and Bailey, C. (1996). Non-pharmacological intervention for breathlessness in lung cancer. *Palliative Medicine*, 10, 299–305.

DH (2003). *Building on the Best: Choice, Responsiveness and Equity in the NHS*. London: DH.

DH (2004) *It Takes Your Breath Away: The Impact of COPD*. CMO Annual Report. Available at www.dh.gov.uk, accessed 14.3.07.

Dow, J.A. and Mest, C.G. (1997). Psychosocial interventions for patients with chronic obstructive pulmonary disease. *Home Healthcare Nurse*, 15(6), 414–420.

Edmonds, P., Khan, S. and Addlington-Hall, J. (2001). A comparison of the palliative care needs of patients dying from chronic respiratory diseases and lung cancer. *Palliative Medicine*, 15, 287–295.

Elkington, H., White, P., Addington-Hall, J., Higgs, R. and Pettinari, C. (2004). The last year of life of COPD: A qualitative study of symptoms and services. *Respiratory Medicine*, 98(5), 439–445.

Elkington, H., White, P., Addington-Hall, J., Higgs, R. and Edmonds, P. (2005). The healthcare needs of chronic obstructive pulmonary disease patients in the last year of life. *Palliative Medicine*, 19(6), 485–491.

Elkington, H., White, P., Higgs, R. and Pettinari, C.J. (2001). GPs' views of prognosis in severe COPD. *Family Practice*, 18(4), 440–444.

Ernst, E., Resch, K.L. and Mills, S. (1995). Complementary medicine: A definition. *British Journal of General Practice*, 45, 506.

Ewing, G., Rogers, M., Barclay, S., McCabe, J. and Martin, A. (2004). Recruiting patients into a primary care-based study of palliative care: Why is it so difficult? *Palliative Medicine*, 18, 452–459.

Ferreira, I.M., Brooks, D., Lacasse, Y., Goldstein, R.S. and White, J. (2005). Nutritional supplementation for stable chronic obstructive pulmonary disease (Cochrane Review). *The Cochrane Library*, 2.

Filshie, J. and White, A. (2005). Complementary medicine for respiratory diseases. In *Supportive Care in Respiratory Disease*, ed S.H. Ahmedzai and M.F. Muers. Oxford: Oxford University Press.

Fletcher, C.M., Elmes, P.C., Fairbairn, M.B. and Wood, C.H. (1959). The significance of respiratory symptoms and the diagnosis of chronic bronchitis in a working population. *British Medical Journal*, 2, 257–266.

Fuld, J.P., Kilduff, L.P., Neder, J.A., Pitsiladis, Y., Lean, M.E., Ward, S.A. and Cotton, M.M. (2005). Creatine supplementation during pulmonary rehabilitation in chronic obstructive pulmonary disease. *Thorax*, 60(7), 531–537.

Gaber, K.A., Barnett, M., Planchant, Y. and Mcgavin, C.R. (2004). Attitudes of 100 patients with COPD to artificial ventilation and cardiopulmonary resuscitation. *Palliative Medicine*, 18, 626–629.

General Medical Service (2006). Revision of the GMS Contract 2006–7: Delivering investment in general practice. Available at www.nhsemployers.org, accessed 1.8.07.

Golin, C.E., Wegner, N.S. and Liu, H. (2000). A prospective study of patient-physician communication about resuscitation. *Journal of the American Geriatrics Society*, 48 (Suppl. 5), S52–S60.

Gore, J.M., Brophy, C.J. and Greenstone, M.A. (2000). How well do we care for patients with end-stage Chronic Obstructive Pulmonary Disease? A comparison of palliative care and quality of life in COPD and lung cancer. *Thorax*, 55, 1000–1006.

Grande, G.E. and Todd, C.J. (2000). Why are trials in palliative care so difficult? *Palliative Medicine*, 14, 69–74.

Griffiths, T.L. and Proud, D. (2005). Creatine supplementation as an exercise performance enhancer for patients with COPD? An idea to run with. *Thorax*, 60(7), 525–526.

Guo, R., Puller, M.H. and Ernst, E. (2006). Herbal medicines for the treatment of COPD: A systematic review. *European Respiratory Journal*, 28(2), 330–338.

Guthrie, S.J., Hill, K.M. and Muers, M.F. (2001). Living with severe COPD. *Respiratory Medicine*, 95, 196–204.

Hately, J., Laurence, V., Scott, A., Baker, R. and Thomas, P. (2003). Breathlessness clinics within specialist palliative care settings can improve the quality of life and functional capacity of patients with lung cancer. *Palliative Medicine*, 17, 410–417.

Healthcare Commission (2006) Clearing the Air. Available at www.healthcarecommission.org.uk, accessed 1.8.07.

Heffner, J.E., Fahy, B., Hilling, L. and Barbieri, C. (1997). Outcomes of advanced directive education of pulmonary rehabilitation patients. *American Journal of Respiratory and Critical Care Medicine*, 155, 1055–1059.

Heslop, K. and Rao, S. (2003). Cognitive behavioural therapy for patients with respiratory disease. *The Airways Journal*, 1(3), 139–141.

Hopkinson, J.B., Wright, D.N.M. and Corner, J. (2005). Seeking new methodology for palliative care research: Challenging assumptions about studying people who are approaching the end of life. *Palliative Medicine*, 19, 532–537.

House of Lords Select Committee for Science and Technology (2000) 6th Report: Complementary and Alternative Medicine. Available at www.publications.parliament.uk, accessed 1.8.07.

Jennings, A.L., Davies, A.N., Higgins, J.P.T. and Broadley, K. (2003). Opioids for the palliation of breathlessness in terminal illness (Cochrane Review). *The Cochrane Library*, 3.

Jones, P.W., Quirk, F.H., Baveystock, C.M. and Littlejohns, P. (1992). A self-complete measure of health status for chronic airflow limitation. *American Review of Respiratory Disease*, 145(6), 1321–1327.

Knauft, E., Nielsen, E.L., Engelberg, R.A., Patrick, D.L. and Curtis, J.R. (2005). Barriers and facilitators to end-of-life care communication for patients with COPD. *Chest*, 127(6), 2188–2196.

Krishnasamy, M., Corner, J., Bredin, M., Plant, H. and Bailey, C. (2001). Cancer nursing practice development: Understanding breathlessness. *Journal of Clinical Nursing*, 10(1), 103–108.

Landbo, C., Prescott, E., Lange, P., Vestbo, J. and Almdal, T.P. (1999). Prognostic value of nutritional status in COPD. *American Journal of Respiratory and Critical Care Medicine*, 160, 1856–1861.

Liverpool Care of the Dying Pathway (LCP) (2005). www.lcp-mariecurie.org.uk

Lynn, J., Ely, E.W., Zhong, Z., McNiff, K.L., Dawson, N.V., Connors, A., Desbiens, N.A., Claessens, M. and McCarthy, E.P. (2000). Living and dying with COPD. *Journal of the American Geriatrics Society*, 48(5, Suppl.), S91–S100.

Maa, S., Gauthier, D. and Turner, M. (1997) Acupressure as an adjunct to a pulmonary rehabilitation program. *Journal of Cardiopulmonary Rehabilitation*, 17, 268–276.

Madge, S. and Esmond, G. (2001). End stage management in respiratory disease. In *Respiratory Nursing*, ed. G. Esmond. London: Harcourt.

Monninkhof, E.M., van der Valk, P.D.L.P.M., van der Palan, J., van der Herwaarden, C. and Partridge, M.R. (2003). Self-management education for patients with COPD: A systematic review. *Thorax*, 58(5), 394–398.

Muers, M.F. (2002). Opioids for dyspnoea. *Thorax*, 57, 922–923.

Muers, M.F. (2005) Diffuse airway obstruction and 'restrictive' lung disease. In *Supportive Care in Respiratory Disease*, ed. S.H. Ahmededzai. Oxford: Oxford University Press.

Murphy, R., Mackway-Jones, K., Sammy, I., Driscoll, P., Gray, A., O'Driscoll, R., O'Reilly, J., Niven, R., Bentley, A., Brear, G. and Kishen, R. (2001). Emergency oxygen therapy for the breathless patient. Guidelines prepared by the North West Oxygen Group. *Emergency Medical Journal*, 18, 421–423.

Murray, S.A., Boyd, K. and Shiekh, A. (2005). Palliative care in chronic illness. *British Medical Journal*, 330, 611–612.

NHS Confederation (2004). Investing in General Practice: The new General Medical Services Contract. Available at www.nhsconfed.org, accessed 5.12.05.

National Institute for Health and Clinical Excellence (NICE) (2004a). Guidelines for the management of COPD. *Thorax*, 59 (Suppl. 1), S1–S232.

National Institute for Health and Clinical Excellence (NICE) (2004b). Improving supportive and palliative care for adults with cancer. Available at www.nice.org.uk, accessed 1.8.07.

Rhodes, P. (1999). Palliative care: The situation of people with chronic respiratory disease. *British Journal of Community Nursing*, 4(3), 131–136.

Ring, L. and Danielson, E. (1997). Patients' experiences of long-term oxygen therapy. *Journal of Advanced Nursing*, 26, 337–344.

Robinson, T. (2005). Living with severe hypoxic COPD: The patient's experience. *Nursing Times*, 101(7), 38–42.

Schols, A.M., Slangen, J., Volovics, L. and Wouters, E.F. (1998). Weight loss is a reversible factor in the prognosis of COPD. *American Journal of Respiratory and Critical Care Medicine*, 157, 1791–1797.

Schols, A.M. and Wouters, E.F. (2000). Nutritional abnormalities and supplementation in COPD. *Clinics in Chest Medicine*, 21, 753–762.

Schwartzstein, R.M., Lahive, K., Pope, A., Weinberger, S.E. and Weiss, J.W. (1987). Cold facial stimulation reduces breathlessness induced in normal subjects. *American Review of Respiratory Diseases*, 136, 58–61.

Seamark, D.A., Blake, S.D., Seamark, C.J. and Halpin, D.M. (2004). Living with Severe Chronic Obstructive Pulmonary Disease: Perceptions of patients and their carers. An interpretive phenomenological analysis. *Palliative Medicine*, 18(7), 619–625.

Sepúlveda, C., Marlin, A., Yoshida, T. and Ullrich, A. (2002). Palliative care: The World Health Organization's global perspective. *Journal of Pain and Symptom Management*, 24(2), 91–96.

Shee, C.D. and Green, M. (2003). Non-invasive ventilation and palliation: Experience in a district general hospital and a review. *Palliative Medicine*, 17, 21–26.

Singh, S.J., Sodergren, S.C., Hyland, M.E., Williams, J. and Morgan, M.D.L. (2001). A comparison of three disease-specific and two generic health-status measures to evaluate the outcome of pulmonary rehabilitation in COPD. *Respiratory Medicine*, 95(1), 71–77.

Skilbeck, J., Mott, L., Page, H., Smith, D., Hjelmeland-Ahmedzai, S. and Clark, D. (1998). Palliative care in COPD: A needs assessment. *Palliative Medicine*, 12, 245–254.

Small, S. and Lamb, M. (1999). Fatigue in chronic illness: The experiences of individuals with COPD and asthma. *Journal of Advanced Nursing*, 30(2), 469–478.

Snaith, R.P. and Zigmond, A.S. (1994). *Hospital Anxiety and Depression Scale*. Windsor: NFER-Nelson.

Stevenson, J.C. and Calverley, P.M.A. (2004). Effect of oxygen on recovery from maximal exercise in patients with obstructive pulmonary disease. *Thorax*, 59, 668–672.

Sullivan, K.E., Hebert, P.C., Logan, J., O'Conner, A.N. and McNeely, P.D. (1996). What do physicians tell patients with end-stage COPD about intubation and mechanical ventilation? *Chest*, 109, 258–264.

Tebbit, P. (1999). *Palliative Care 2000: Commissioning through Partnership*. Northampton: National Council for Hospice and Specialist Palliative Care Services, Land and Unwin (Data Sciences)

Trendall, J. (2000). Concept analysis: Chronic fatigue. *Journal of Advanced Nursing*, 32(5), 1126–1131.

Weinman, J OTHER AUTHORS (1984). *Measures in Health Psychology: A User's Portfolio*. Windsor: NFER-Nelson.

Wilkinson, I.S., Prigmore, S. and Rayner, C.F. (2006). A randomised-controlled trial examining the effects of reflexology on patients with chronic obstructive pulmonary disease (COPD). *Complementary Therapies in Clinical Practice*, 12(2), 141–147.

Williams, S.J. and Bury, M.R. (1989). Impairment, disability and handicap in chronic respiratory illness. *Social Science and Medicine*, 29(5), 609–616.

Wong, Q. and Bourbeau, J. (2005). Outcomes and health-related quality of life following hospitalisation for an acute exacerbation of COPD. *Respirology*, 10(3), 334–340.

Chapter 10
Domiciliary oxygen therapy
Dave Lynes

Domiciliary oxygen therapy can be in the form of long-term oxygen therapy (LTOT), ambulatory oxygen therapy and short burst therapy.

Long-Term Oxygen Therapy (LTOT)

Long-Term Oxygen Therapy

Long-Term Oxygen Therapy (LTOT) is an important intervention. If it is given to a compliant person with COPD who has been assessed and deemed eligible, it has the potential to prolong life significantly. Two landmark trials (MRC, 1981; NOTT, 1980) showed that use of low concentration oxygen for 15 hours a day in severe COPD improved survival, reduced secondary polycythaemia, improved sleep quality and neurophysiological functioning and improved blood flow to the kidneys.

As COPD becomes more severe, a lack of oxygen in the alveoli causes changes in the pulmonary blood circulation which culminates in the development of pulmonary hypertension and right-sided heart failure. This is called cor pulmonale. Cor pulmonale can significantly reduce life expectancy in a COPD patient; therefore oxygenation of the alveoli is important. Eligible patients should be prescribed LTOT for a minimum of 15 hours a day but survival improves when it is used for more than 20 hours a day. This should include night time, because hypoxaemia can worsen during sleep (NICE, 2004). Once started, LTOT is likely to be life-long.

In order for patients to benefit from LTOT they should be chronically hypoxic. Oxygen concentrators are normally provided and these use the household electrical supply. Although oxygen can be delivered through a mask, nasal cannulae are preferred.

This is because they enable patients to talk, eat and drink. When fitted, tubing of up to 50 feet restricts movements as little as possible. Flow rate on oxygen concentrators can be adjusted, and it must be sufficient to raise the patient's arterial oxygen tension above 8 kPa whilst they are awake.

It is important that a patient is assessed for LTOT prior to prescribing it. There is no evidence that domiciliary oxygen therapy is useful for those who are not hypoxic. Moreover it is expensive and can significantly restrict a patient's lifestyle, so it is important to ensure that only those who are eligible for the therapy receive it (MRC, 1981; NOTT, 1980). Before assessing the need for LTOT, ensure that the patient has the correct diagnosis. They should also have 'optimum' medical management of their COPD in that their pharmacological management should be correct, and this needs to have been the case for several weeks. They should have been clinically stable for approximately five weeks prior to the assessment, as an exacerbation can result in a lower than normal PaO_2 which may mean that the patient is prescribed LTOT when they do not need it. It is important, therefore, not to assess for LTOT during an admission to hospital for an exacerbation.

To be eligible for LTOT prescription, the patients PaO_2 should be at or below 7.3 kPa when breathing air. LTOT can also be prescribed when the PaO_2 is between 7.3 and 8 kPa if the patient also has secondary polycythaemia or evidence of pulmonary hypertension (BTS, 2006). Blood gases should be measured twice, not less than three weeks apart, and when the patient is in a period of clinical stability. It is important to ensure that the patient has been breathing air for at least 30 minutes before samples are obtained for blood gas analysis.

Once the decision has been made to prescribe LTOT, you need to establish the patient's response to it. This is to ensure that the oxygen therapy is sufficient to raise the patient's arterial oxygen tension above 8 kPa whilst they are awake. Supplemental oxygen flow rate of two litres a minute is usual, but if this is insufficient the flow rate should be increased gradually and the patient left on the increased flow rate for at least 30 minutes before obtaining a sample for gas analysis.

It is essential to measure blood gases rather than SaO_2 by using a pulse oximeter. This is because some COPD patients may develop clinically-significant hypercapnia, and pulse oximetry would not provide this information. A pulse oximeter would nevertheless be useful in a primary care setting, because it might enable practitioners to identify those patients who require assessment for LTOT (when SaO_2 is less than 92 per cent whilst breathing room air and at rest).

The most common site for obtaining a sample for blood gas analysis is the radial artery, although the brachial or femoral arteries can be used should circulation in any of these areas be poor. This can be a painful procedure for the patient. As an alternative, arterialised capillary blood samples can be taken, usually from the ear lobe. This can be achieved by rubbing the earlobe with a vasodilator cream, ensuring a rapid flow of blood through the capillary. A small nick will allow blood to ooze out which can be collected in a fine capillary tube and then analysed immediately, taking care not to introduce any air. It has been found that $PaCO_2$ results are within 0.1 kPa and pH is the same when compared to arterial blood (Zavorsky *et al.*, 2007).

It may be that a patient does not fulfil the criteria for prescription of LTOT but their gases are borderline. If this is the case, it would be appropriate to repeat the assessment at some point in the future, perhaps three months later.

For LTOT to work, the patient has to be compliant. They have to use the oxygen therapy correctly for at least 15 hours a day, including nocturnal use. There are many reasons why a patient may be non-compliant. They may not understand the reason for LTOT and may think that they do not need to use it if they do not feel breathless. They may also experience problems such as sore ears and nose and the noise from the concentrator may make patients reluctant to use it at night. Education and written information is therefore essential, and follow-up visits are important if problems are to be identified. The patient's family or carer should also be given full information.

The patient should understand that they need to take the LTOT for at least 15 hours a day and they should know why it has been prescribed. They should understand how to operate the oxygen concentrator or the ambulatory oxygen device and they should have a basic understanding of some of the principles of oxygen therapy, such as the importance of not adjusting flow rate. The basics do need to be explained, including what might seem obvious. For example, patients with nasal cannulae often mouth breathe, not realising that they will need to breathe through their nose in order to inhale the oxygen.

The patient should also have an engineer's contact number should the oxygen concentrator break down, and understand how to use a back-up cylinder. A contact number for a respiratory specialist practitioner may also be helpful. Importantly, the dangers of smoking whilst using LTOT equipment should be emphasised. Oxygen supports combustion and smoking whilst using LTOT is a significant fire risk.

In the UK, patients should be followed up with a home visit within a month, and should return to hospital or to a specialist community service for reassessment approximately three months after starting LTOT. Follow-ups are an opportunity to establish whether there is good compliance and to deal with any problems that the patient may be experiencing. They are also an opportunity to educate the patient, check their understanding and reiterate salient points. It is important to ensure that home LTOT is adequately correcting hypoxemia and that the patient still needs it (Restrick et $al.$, 1993). Recording SaO_2 with pulse oximetry whilst on LTOT at the prescribed flow rate should provide evidence of satisfactory correction of hypoxemia; the SaO_2 should be at 92 per cent or above. If LTOT is not correcting hypoxaemia the patient should be referred to a specialist service for reassessment.

It is also important to measure SaO_2 after the patient has been breathing air for at least half an hour. If the patient's SaO_2 is 92 per cent or above whilst breathing air, the SaO_2 should be checked again in approximately one month, and if it remains 92 per cent or above the patient should be referred for review by the specialist service to assess the continued requirement for LTOT (BTS, 2006). During the assessment visit arterial blood gas measurements should be taken while the patient is breathing air and while they are breathing oxygen therapy at the prescribed flow rate. Reassessment is also important if the patient's condition deteriorates or if there is evidence of worsening hypercapnia. Evidence for this might be if they are suffering from morning headaches.

Ambulatory oxygen therapy

Ambulatory oxygen therapy

The annual cost of an oxygen concentrator is less than that of cylinders and it is more convenient because cylinders need delivering and changing. However, the oxygen concentrator is not portable and it will restrict the patient to their home environment during LTOT. Ambulatory oxygen therapy can help in this respect and is usually prescribed for those who are mobile and who leave the home regularly. There are a range of portable devices including portable cylinders, cylinders with oxygen conserving devices and liquid oxygen. The devices vary in cost and weight, so careful selection of a device that meets the patient's specific needs is important. It is helpful to determine the amount of outside activity that the patient is likely to engage in. Clearly a housebound patient will need less ambulatory oxygen every day than a patient who visits relatives daily. It should only be prescribed after assessment and this usually involves access to a hospital specialist.

Ambulatory oxygen therapy is important to ensure that some patients are able to be compliant with LTOT but it is also useful for those who do not require LTOT because they have normal arterial oxygen levels at rest but desaturate during exercise. Desaturation during exercise is defined as a reduction in SaO_2 of four per cent to a value less than 90 per cent (Eaton *et al.*, 2002). Assessment for ambulatory oxygen therapy can therefore involve exercise tests such as a shuttle walk test or a six minute walking test (McDonald *et al.*, 1995) with a pulse oximeter in place. Assessment may also involve the use of diary cards, to establish the appropriateness of a specific device for an individual patient's lifestyle.

Short Burst Oxygen Therapy

Short Burst Oxygen Therapy

Short burst oxygen therapy is different to LTOT and ambulatory oxygen therapy. It is the occasional use of oxygen at home and it is prescribed to relieve the sensation of breathlessness that is not relieved by other therapy. Although short burst oxygen therapy is extensively prescribed, there is little evidence that it is effective (Smith *et al.*, 2003; Stevenson & Calverley, 2004) although patients do report subjective benefit.

Patients typically use it intermittently for periods of approximately 10 minutes. Some patients use it to pre-oxygenate themselves before exercise and may use it during and after exercise whilst recovering. Sometimes short burst oxygen therapy is prescribed on discharge from hospital following an exacerbation of COPD. This prescription is normally followed by an LTOT assessment.

There is no specific method of assessment for the prescription of short burst therapy. The British Thoracic Society working group on home oxygen services (BTS, 2006) has recommended that other causes of breathlessness must be excluded and the patient should report subjective improvement if short burst therapy is to be continued. All patients on short burst oxygen therapy should be seen at least once a year by their primary care physician or specialist to review the continuing need for the short burst oxygen. It may also be necessary to assess for LTOT.

Domiciliary oxygen therapy is a long-established intervention but guidelines and recommendations are constantly changing. This chapter is an introduction to basic concepts.

For current guidelines visit the British Thoracic Society website (www.brit-thoracic.org.uk).

References

British Thoracic Society (BTS) (2006). *Clinical Component for the Home Oxygen Service in England and Wales.* London: BTS.

Eaton, T., Garrett, J.E. and Young, P. (2002). Ambulatory oxygen improves quality of life of COPD patients: A randomised controlled study. *European Respiratory Journal*, 20, 306–312.

McDonald, C.F., Blyth, C.M., Lazarus, M.D., Marschner, I. and Barter, C.E. (1995). Exertional oxygen of limited benefit in patients with chronic obstructive pulmonary disease and mild hypoxaemia. *American Journal of Respiratory and Critical Care Medicine*, 152, 1616–1619.

Medical Research Council (MRC) (1981). Long-term domiciliary oxygen therapy in chronic hypoxic cor pulmonale complicating chronic bronchitis and emphysema. *Lancet*, 1, 681–686.

National Institute for Health and Clinical Excellence (NICE) (2004). Chronic Obstructive Pulmonary Disease. National clinical guideline on management of chronic obstructive pulmonary disease in adults in primary and secondary care. Guideline 12. *Thorax*, 59 (Suppl. 1), S1–S232.

National Patient Safety Agency (NPSA) (2004). Achieving our Aims: Evaluating the results of the pilot Clean Your Hands campaign. Available at www.npsa.nhs.uk/cleanyourhands, accessed 24.1.07.

NOTT (1980). Continuous or nocturnal oxygen therapy in hypoxaemic chronic obstructive lung disease. *Annals of Internal Medicine*, 93, 391–398.

Restrick, L.J., Paul, E.A., Braid, G.M., Cullinan, P., Moore-Gillon, J. and Wedzicha, J.A. (1993) Assessment and follow-up of patients prescribed long-term oxygen treatment. *Thorax*, 48, 708–713.

Smith, A.A., Crawford, A., MacRae, K.D., Garrod, R., Seed, W.A. and Roberts, C.M. (2003). Oxygen supplementation before or after submaximal exercise in patients with chronic obstructive pulmonary disease. *Thorax*, 58, 670–673.

Stevenson, N.J. and Calverley, M.A. (2004). Effect of oxygen on recovery from maximal exercise in patients with chronic obstructive pulmonary disease. *Thorax*, 59, 668–672.

Zavorsky, G., Cao, J., Mayo, N., Gabbay, R. and Murias, J. (2007). Arterial versus capillary blood gases: A meta-analysis. *Respiratory Physiology & Neurobiology*, 155(3), 268–279.

Chapter 11
Pulmonary rehabilitation
Carol Kelly

Pulmonary rehabilitation is defined as a multidisciplinary programme of care for patients with chronic respiratory impairment that is individually designed to optimise the individual's physical and social performance and autonomy (BTS, 2001).

The progressive and insidious nature of COPD often results in learned behaviour by patients, whereby patients adapt their lifestyle in order to accommodate breathlessness and avoid the terrifying experiences that becoming unduly breathless can cause. This adaptation then contributes to a lowering of fitness level and disability, which in turn may lead to unemployment, social isolation and further inactivity – a vicious cycle often referred to as a downward spiral of inactivity (Figure 11.1).

Figure 11.1

The cycle of decline in COPD

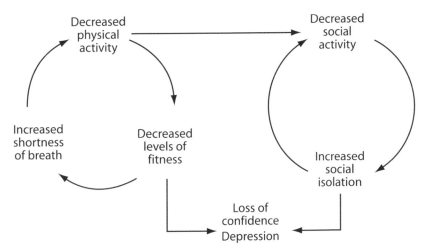

The consequence for the patient is not only debilitating physiological symptoms, predominantly breathlessness, but also many psychosocial effects from living with the disease. Exercise tolerance itself is affected by other factors including ventilatory limitation, gas exchange limitations, cardiac dysfunction, skeletal and respiratory muscle dysfunction and nutritional status, which demonstrates the systemic manifestations and complexities of the disease pathology. The main disabling manifestation of the disease is dyspnoea, which is a perception of breathlessness, closely interrelated with anxiety (Brenes, 2003), that needs to be considered as a subjective patient view.

It is these self-perpetuating, negative feedback mechanisms that pulmonary rehabilitation ultimately seeks to address.

Background

Background

An increasing recognition of the importance of quality of life and health status in COPD has highlighted the importance of pulmonary rehabilitation as an effective intervention in the management of this potentially debilitating disease. The aim of pulmonary rehabilitation is to lessen the impact of symptoms and, within the limits of the disability, restore as much normal function as possible. This is achieved through an exercise training programme but additionally by 'normalising' dyspnoea; breath-lessness is a normal response to exercise and within a pulmonary rehabilitation setting patients are often, for the first time, given permission to become breathless.

Pulmonary rehabilitation has been popular in the US for some years but has only recently become widely accepted in the UK. It is now highlighted as a priority in the organisation and delivery of care (NICE, 2004; DH, 2004). Evidence-based support for pulmonary rehabilitation has grown tremendously and it has been clearly demonstrated to reduce dyspnoea, increase exercise performance and improve health-related quality of life (ATS/ERS, 2006). A recent systematic review also identified that rehabilita-tion improves emotional function and enhances patients' sense of control over their condition (Lacasse *et al.*, 2006). In addition, a reduction in healthcare utilisation (Troosters *et al.*, 2005) supports the cost-effectiveness of pulmonary rehabilitation as a management strategy. Together with recent advances in the understanding of the pathophysiology of COPD this evidence base is enabling pulmonary rehabilitation programmes to be extended in scope and application.

Goals and principles

There are British guidelines in the form of a statement published in 2001 by the British Thoracic Society (BTS) that sets out key points regarding selection, setting programme content, process and outcome measures.

The general principles of pulmonary rehabilitation are described as follows:

- The goals of rehabilitation are to reduce the symptoms, disability and handicap and to improve functional independence in people with lung disease.
- It is assumed that optimum medical management has been achieved or continues alongside the rehabilitation process.
- The rehabilitation process incorporates a programme of physical training, disease education, nutritional support, psychological, social and behavioural intervention.
- Rehabilitation is provided by a multidisciplinary team with involvement of the patients' family and attention to individual needs.
- The outcome of rehabilitation for individuals and programmes should be continually observed with the appropriate measures of impairment, disability and handicap.

(BTS, 2001)

The NICE guidelines on the management of COPD (2004) offer the following recommendations.

- Pulmonary rehabilitation should be made available to all appropriate patients with COPD.
- Pulmonary rehabilitation should be offered to all patients who consider themselves functionally disabled by COPD (usually MRC grade 3 and above). Pulmonary rehabilitation is not suitable for patients who are unable to walk, have unstable angina or who have had a recent myocardial infarction.
- For pulmonary rehabilitation programmes to be effective, and to improve concordance, they should be held at times that suit patients, and in buildings that are easy for patients to get to and have good access for people with disabilities. Places should be available within a reasonable time of referral.
- Pulmonary rehabilitation programmes should include multi-component, multidisciplinary interventions, which are tailored

to the individual patient's needs. The rehabilitation process should incorporate a programme of physical training, disease education, nutritional, psychological and behavioural intervention.

- Patients should be made aware of the benefits of pulmonary rehabilitation and the commitment required to gain these.

(NICE, 2004)

The American Thoracic Society and European Thoracic Society issued a joint statement in 2006 further highlighting the importance of pulmonary rehabilitation as an integral management strategy for most chronic respiratory diseases and stated that it should not be viewed as a 'last ditch' effort for patients with severe respiratory impairment (ATS/ERS, 2006).

Typical components of a pulmonary rehabilitation programme include exercise and education sessions and may include specific interventions such as smoking cessation. Additionally psycho-social support is integrated within programmes in both a formal manner, such as giving advice on benefits, and informally through social integration.

Setting and organisation of pulmonary programmes

Pulmonary programmes

Traditionally these programmes have been located in secondary care as an out-patient service, partly because it was specialist physicians, nurses and physiotherapists that initiated schemes and because of the availability of the multidisciplinary team. This has caused problems for patients, not least of which is access and in particular parking. More recently community-based programmes have been developed and the evidence has been positive. The BTS (2001) concluded that pulmonary rehabilitation is effective in all settings including hospital in-patient, hospital out-patient, the community and even at home.

Duration of programmes

Duration

The optimum duration of programmes has not been as extensively researched as programme content or setting although it is generally believed that longer programmes produce larger, more enduring training effects (ATS/ERS, 2006). The benefits gained from attending a programme appear to wane with time (Foglio *et al.*, 1999). However, evidence is emerging that attendance at further pulmonary rehabilitation programmes or follow-up does result in sustained improvements (Foglio *et al.*, 2001).

Patient selection

Patient selection

The NICE guidelines (2004) suggest that pulmonary rehabilitation is offered to all patients considered functionally disabled by their breathlessness. The MRC dyspnoea scale (see Chapter 4) offers a simple, quick and easy-to-use tool, suitable for any clinical setting, that attempts to measure the subjective experience of dyspnoea in an objective manner. Anything over MRC 3 ('I walk slower than other people of the same age when walking at my own pace on the level') is considered as a functional disability.

Other criteria for selection usually require the patient to be clinically stable, on optimum medication and without any other physical disability that would prevent exercise. In addition, the patient must be well-motivated. Without this impetus pulmonary rehabilitation will not be successful.

Conventionally lung function, notably FEV_1, was used as the principal outcome measure for assessing effectiveness of most interventions for COPD. Now, in the light of evidence indicating that changes in symptoms and quality of life can occur independently of changes in lung function, and supporting a symptom-based palliative approach to managing COPD, other outcomes, such as health-related quality of life, are considered equally valuable measures.

Assessment

Assessment

Assessment usually involves the patient attending prior to commencing the programme for a series of objective physical tests and a subjective assessment of their quality of life.

Exercise testing

The exercise test serves to not only assess the patient's functional ability prior to commencing pulmonary rehabilitation but also to determine an exercise endurance pace that is specific to them. Additionally it can serve to reinforce to the patient that exercise is within their capabilities. Many patients are either frightened, sceptical or even disbelieving that exercise may help them to manage their disease and control their dyspnoea; by this stage most have gradually been reducing their daily function in order to accommodate it.

Exercise tests can be done in the laboratory using equipment such as treadmills or cycle ergometer tests while wearing a face mask or mouthpiece and nose clips to provide gas analysis. However such tests are not widely available, the equipment is expensive and the procedure unpleasant for the patient. Therefore, field tests have now been developed and are much more practical in most clinical settings. These tests are either self-paced or externally-paced and are usually conducted at assessment pre- and post-programme in order to measure any improvement (Singh *et al.*, 1992).

Self-paced tests

The most commonly used self-paced test is the six-minute walk test in which patients are required to walk as far as possible in six minutes.

Externally-paced tests

A common externally-paced test is the shuttle-walking test. This uses a pre-recorded series of beeps. The patient is required to walk around a ten-metre course, usually set up with traffic cones. The test is incremental allowing an objective assessment of maximum functional ability.

Quality of life

Quality of life is the patient's subjective judgement of their health status and can be assessed by interview or by question-naire. There are many validated tools available now to assess quality of life and these are either generic or disease-specific; one such example is the St George's Respiratory Questionnaire (Jones *et al.*, 1992).

Exercise training

Exercise training is an integral and essential component of any pulmonary rehabilitation programme. Through training, fitness levels are addressed and the patient's confidence in both exercising and managing breathlessness is increased.

Types of exercise

- Aerobic – typically walking or exercise bike. There is a great deal of evidence that shows that this type of training improves exercise tolerance and health status in patients with COPD. Patients are required to complete at least three episodes of

Exercise training

training a week for 20 to 30 minutes, of which at least two should be supervised (BTS, 2001).

- Lower limb training – This appears to improve functional capacity and exercise endurance through addressing deconditioning of muscles.
- Upper limb training – This may be important because of the way patients with COPD breathe and the effects of hyper-inflation. They often use the upper body to assist in the work of breathing. Arm training can therefore improve exercise performance by decreasing ventilatory demand during arm work, making everyday tasks such as washing hair, pegging out washing and gardening – activities patients often complain about experiencing difficulties with – much easier.

Physiotherapy

The physiotherapist plays an important role in pulmonary rehabilitation by both leading the exercise component of the programme (although non-medical exercise instructors have now begun to be used for this) and teaching sputum clearance and breathing control techniques.

Sputum clearance

Sputum production often increases during exacerbations and it is important that the patient is able to remove this as effectively and efficiently as possible to avoid worsening dyspnoea and exhaustion. The active cycle of breathing (Webber & Pryor, 1993) consists of controlled breathing, deep breathing (three or four relaxed deep breaths) followed by the 'huff' – a forced but gentle expiration with an open mouth that uses abdominal contraction to expel the air. The huff requires less effort than a cough and, when performed correctly, does not increase airways obstruction.

Breathing techniques

Dyspnoea is usually the most important symptom for COPD patients and successful control can cause significant improvements in both physical and psychological comfort. Breathing control is taught in the controlled pulmonary rehabilitation setting. Learning techniques in this controlled environment enables patients to build their confidence and utilise the techniques during periods of extreme breathlessness caused by anxiety or exercise.

Breathing control allows the patient to function more slowly, but more comfortably, for longer, without needing a long recovery period after activity. Timing breathing to a rhythm can also be helpful (for example, for climbing steps). During all physical activity patients are taught to exhale during the exertion part of the movement and inhale during the relaxation phase.

Position is also important. The lean forward position increases the diaphragm's force of contraction and supports the shoulder girdle, so optimising movement of the thoracic cage. This position can be adopted either sitting or standing. Some patients also find aids such as walking sticks useful to lean on when out walking; window shopping is another commonly-adapted strategy for recovery.

Educational component

Educational component

Patient education to date has not been proved to be effective as a single component in COPD management (Monninkhof *et al.*, 2003). However, it has become a central feature of pulmonary rehabilitation programmes. (See 'Education' in Chapter 9 for the areas commonly covered.) The form and delivery of these sessions will depend on local resources and availability of speakers. Often sessions are reinforced with the use of leaflets and educational materials.

Specific interventions

In addition to the general content some specific interventions can also be incorporated. These may include psychological and behavioural interventions such as cognitive behavioural therapy (Heslop & Rao, 2003). Anxiety and depression can also be improved by rehabilitation (Withers *et al.*, 1999). Most healthcare professionals involved in pulmonary rehabilitation would advocate that psychological and behavioural intervention is embedded in the structure of the programmes through the delivery of education, small group discussions and relaxation therapy, in addition to the positive ethos that rehabilitation instils.

Nutrition

Weight loss is common in people with COPD, especially as their disease progresses and increasingly nutritional depletion with cachexia and muscle wasting are recognised as features of severe COPD (Schols & Wouters, 2000). Whether this is a consequence or contributing cause of severity is unclear. Weight loss, in particular loss of fat-free mass (including skeletal muscle), occurs if energy expenditure exceeds dietary intake and muscle wasting is a consequence of this. In addition, ageing itself can cause muscle wasting, a process known as sarcopenia, further compounding the COPD processes in many elderly patients.

There is now a growing body of evidence that suggests that nutritional supplementation augments exercise by increasing muscle mass (Fuld *et al.*, 2005; Griffiths & Proud, 2005) and there is clearly a need for further research in this area. Ongoing research is exploring how nutritional support can enhance exercise training and optimise the effects of pulmonary rehabilitation. It appears that the gold standard will be a combination of both exercise and nutritional support.

Oxygen

Patients who are receiving long-term oxygen therapy continue with it during exercise training but may need increased flow rates. Oxygen supplementation as an adjunct to exercise training has recently attracted interest. The evidence has specifically investigated oxygen supplementation in two specific groups: those who desaturate with exercise and those who do not (Garrod *et al.*, 2000). Evidence suggests that using oxygen allows higher training intensities and enhanced exercise performance even without desaturation, probably mediated by a reduced ventilatory response (O'Donnell *et al.*, 2001; Emtner *et al.*, 2003). However, it is still unclear whether this translates into improved clinical outcomes and further studies in this area are needed before routine use can be recommended. More recently the use of heliox, a mixture of oxygen and helium, has also proved to reduce air-trapping and enhance exercise tolerance in COPD (Palange *et al.*, 2005). Although this evidence supports supplementation it will not allow clinicians to predict individual responses and individual assessments may always need to be conducted.

Drug therapy

The possible role of drug therapy in enhancing the effects of pulmonary rehabilitation is also being investigated. Tiotropium, a once-daily inhaled anticholinergic bronchodilator, is of particular interest because of the effects of reduced lung hyperinflation

(Casaburi *et al.*, 2002; O'Donnell *et al.*, 2004). In a double-blind, placebo randomised, controlled trial, tiotropium, together with eight weeks of pulmonary rehabilitation, showed an improved health-related quality of life which was maintained at 12 weeks post-programme, together with a reduction in salbutamol use (Casaburi *et al.*, 2005).

The use of anabolic steroids may also prove beneficial in enhancing the effects of exercise training (Creutzberg *et al.*, 2003), but again results are only preliminary.

Non-invasive ventilation

Non-invasive ventilation techniques have been studied as adjuncts to physical exercise training in COPD both to attain higher levels of intensity of exercise and as a mechanism for resting respiratory muscles between exercise periods. Although potentially promising the small, unblinded studies so far cannot inform clinical practice and further investigation is needed (Troosters *et al.*, 2005).

Early pulmonary rehabilitation

The effects of early pulmonary rehabilitation in the acute recovery phase of an exacerbation have been studied. In a randomised controlled trial, Man *et al.* (2004) demonstrated that this intervention was safe and led to statistically and clinically-significant improvements in exercise capacity and health status at three months. However, the study was unblinded and a placebo effect may have been a principal mechanism for the improvements observed. Larger randomised studies are required.

Patient outcomes

Individual assessment of benefits is an integral part of programmes. Disability can be pragmatically assessed by testing functional capacity with a field-based exercise test and compared with pre-assessment results. A measure of dyspnoea or fatigue should also be considered and will increase the sensitivity of the exercise measurements. Quality of life measurements can also be repeated to detect any improvement.

Overall, although most tools have demonstrated sensitivity to certain aspects of outcomes, none are currently designed specifically for pulmonary rehabilitation and often it is the subjective response of the patients that encompasses benefits more articulately. Anecdotal evidence of such life-changing effects are common, for example: 'pulmonary rehabilitation has changed my life. I can now bend down to work the video player. Previously I had to wait for my wife to come home from work.'

Summary

Pulmonary rehabilitation is an evidence-based intervention in the management of COPD in the short and long term, aimed at improved exercise tolerance, reduced symptoms and improved health-related quality of life, together with a decrease in healthcare utilisation. It has been established as a means of alleviating symptoms and optimising function, independent of the disease progression. However, further research is still needed to evaluate duration, degree of supervision and intensity of training and how long the treatment effects persist.

Once the evidence is well-established and recognised, the widespread implementation of these programmes is needed to ensure consistency and equitable access to services for all COPD patients.

References

American Thoracic Society (ATS)/European Respiratory Society (ERS) (2006). Statement on pulmonary rehabilitation. *American Journal of Respiratory and Critical Care Medicine*, **173**, 1390–1413.

Brenes, G.A. (2003). Anxiety and COPD: Prevalence, impact and treatment. *Psychosomatic Medicine*, **65**, 963–970.

British Thoracic Society (BTS) (2001). BTS Statement on Pulmonary Rehabilitation. British Thoracic Society Standards of Care Sub-committee on Pulmonary Rehabilitation. *Thorax*, **56**(11), 827–834.

Casaburi, R., Mahler, D.A., Jones, P.W., Wanner, A., San Pedro, G., ZuWallack, B. L., Menjoge, S. S., Serby, C. W. and Witek, T. (2002). A long-term evaluation of once-daily inhaled tiotropium in COPD. *European Respiratory Journal*, **19**(2), 217–224.

Casaburi, R., Kukafka, D., Cooper, C.B., Witek, T.D. and Kresten, S. (2005). Improvement in exercise tolerance with the combination of tiotropium and pulmonary rehabilitation in patients with COPD. *Chest*, **127**, 809–817.

Creutzberg, E.C., Wouters, E.F., Mostert, R., Pluymers, R.J., and Schols, A.M. (2003). A role for anabolic steroids in the rehabilitation of patients with COPD? A double-blind, placebo-controlled, randomized trial. *Chest*, **124**, 1733–1742.

DH (2004) It Takes Your Breath Away: The impact of COPD. CMO Annual Report. Available at www.dh.gov.uk, accessed 14.3.07.

Emtner, M., Porszasz, J., Burns, M., Somfay, A. and Casaburi, R. (2003). Benefits of supplemental oxygen in exercise training in nonhypoxaemic COPD patients. *American Journal of Respiratory and Critical Care Medicine*, **168**, 1034–1042.

Foglio, K., Bianchi, L., Bruletti, G., Battista, L., Pagani, M. and Ambrosino, N. (1999). Long-term effectiveness of pulmonary rehabilitation in patients with chronic airway obstruction. *European Respiratory Journal*, **13**, 125–132.

Foglio, K., Bianchi, L. and Ambrosino, N. (2001). Is it really useful to repeat an outpatient pulmonary rehabilitation programme in patients with chronic airway obstruction? A two-year controlled study. *Chest*, **119**, 1696–1704.

Fuld, J.P., Kilduff, L.P., Neder, J.A., Pitsiladis, Y., Lean, M.E., Ward, S.A. and Cotton M.M. (2005). Creatinine supplementation during pulmonary rehabilitation in chronic obstructive pulmonary disease. *Thorax*, **60**(7), 531–537.

Garrod, R., Paul, E.A. and Wedzicha, J.A. (2000). Supplemental oxygen during pulmonary rehabilitation in patients with COPD with exercise hypoxaemia. *Thorax*, **55**, 539–543.

Griffiths, T.L. and Proud, D. (2005). Creatine supplementation as an exercise performance enhancer for patients with COPD? An idea to run with. *Thorax*, **60**(7), 525–526.

Heslop, K. and Rao, S. (2003). Cognitive behavioural therapy for patients with respiratory disease. *The Airways Journal*, **1**(3), 139–141.

Jones, P.W., Quirk, F.H., Bavystock, C.M. and Littlejohns, P. (1992). A self-complete measure for chronic airflow limitation – the St George's Respiratory Questionnaire. *American Review of Respiratory Disease*, 145, 1321–1327.

Lacasse, Y., Goldstein, R., Lasserson, T.J., and Martin, S. (2006). Pulmonary rehabilitation for chronic obstructive pulmonary disease (Cochrane Review). *The Cochrane Library*, 4.

Man, W.D.C., Polkey, M.I., Donaldson, N., Gray, B.J. and Moxham, J. (2004). Community pulmonary rehabilitation after hospitalisation for acute exacerbations of COPD: Randomised controlled study. *British Medical Journal*, 329, 1209.

Monninkhof, E.M., van der Valk, P.D.L.P.M., van der Palan, J., van der Herwaarden, C. and Partridge, M.R. (2003). Self-management education for patients with COPD: A systematic review. *Thorax*, 58(5), 394–398

National Institute for Health and Clinical Excellence (NICE) (2004). Chronic Obstructive Pulmonary Disease: Management of chronic obstructive pulmonary disease in adults in primary and secondary care. Available at www.nice.org.uk, accessed 14.3.07.

O'Donnell, D.E., D'Arsigny, C. and Webb, K.A. (2001). Effects of hyperoxia on ventilatory limits in advanced COPD. *American Journal of Respiratory and Critical Care Medicine*, 163, 892–898.

O'Donnell, D.E., Fluge, T., Gerken, F., Hamilton, A., Webb, K., Aguilaniu, B., Make, B. and Magnussen, H. (2004). Effects of Tiotropium on lung hyperinflation, dyspnoea and exercise tolerance in COPD. *European Respiratory Journal*, 23, 832–840.

Palange, P., Crimi, E., Pellegrino, R. and Brusasco, V. (2005). Supplemental oxygen and heliox: 'New' tools for exercise training in COPD. *Current Opinion in Pulmonary Medicine*, 11, 145–148.

Schols, A.M. and Wouters, E.F. (2000). Nutritional abnormalities and supplementation in COPD. *Clinics in Chest Medicine*, 21, 753–762.

Singh, S., Morgan, M., Scott, S., Walters, D. and Hardman, A. (1992). Development of a shuttle walking test of disability in patients with chronic airways obstruction. *Thorax*, 47(12), 1019–1024.

Troosters, T., Casaburi, R., Gosselink, R. and Decramer, M. (2005). Pulmonary rehabilitation in COPD. *American Journal of Respiratory and Critical Care Medicine*, 172(1), 19–38.

Webber, B.A. and Pryor, J.A. (1993). Physiotherapy skills: Techniques and adjuncts. In *Physiotherapy for Respiratory and Cardiac Problems*, eds B.A. Webber and J.A. Pryor. Edinburgh: Churchill Livingstone.

Withers, N.J., Rudkin, S.T., and White, R.J. (1999). Anxiety and depression in severe COPD: The effects of pulmonary rehabilitation. *Journal of Cardiopulmonary Rehabilitation*, 19, 362–365.

Index